Story and Table

"Mike Roth takes a biblical view that is at once thoughtful, rigorous, and (perhaps most importantly) life-giving. His theology has been a lifeline for me and many others who seek spiritual rhythms grounded in clear-eyed humility, nonviolence, and care for all people. This is a deeply Christian framework that meets the current moment."

—**Vivi Parecki**, Pathologist, Pearl Church since 2023

"*Story and Table* breaks through ideas that have led us far from the teachings of Christ and, most importantly, sends us out to follow Christ with authenticity and love. Mike Roth writes with deep poetic care about ideas that are essential for the contemporary church."

—**Martin French**, Illustrator/Designer/Professor, Pearl Church since 2019

"At the core of this work, Dr. Roth restores the image of 'good.' Anyone who has questioned their Christian identity because of violent and harmful theology will find that Dr. Roth's book is both a salve to old wounds and an invitation back to God's table."

—**Mo Hawthorne**, Lawyer, Pearl Church 2004–2021

"After a lifelong struggle to reconcile an all-loving God with the violent, exclusive salvation preached through evangelical biblical inerrancy, this holistic approach to theology has revealed what I had always known about the Divine: God's desire for humanity is not shame or self-sacrifice, but flourishing. There is no separation from God. I am of God—just as I am today, and just as I will be tomorrow."

—**Eli W.**, Barber, Pearl Church since 2021

"Mike Roth's insightful teachings were a scaffold for me to develop an intelligent delve into Scripture to resolve the cognitive dissonance of evangelical theology without abandoning Christianity. I appreciate the unique way he can present a scholarly approach to deconstruction while maintaining a heartfelt love for the teachings of Jesus and the importance of Christian traditions and community. This book is for the curious who feel stuck with a gnawing knowing that traditional dogma doesn't line up with the inclusive love and peaceful teachings of Jesus. This book maps a journey of an honest scholarly examination of theology while holding onto the heart of Christianity."

—**Valinda Harlan**, Professor of Psychology and Licensed Mental Health Counselor, Pearl Church since 2018

Story and Table

Discovering Hope and Healing
in Evolving Christianity

Mike Roth

FOREWORD BY
David Khalaf

WIPF & STOCK · Eugene, Oregon

STORY AND TABLE
Discovering Hope and Healing in Evolving Christianity

Copyright © 2025 Mike Roth. All rights reserved. Except for brief quotations in critical publications or reviews, no part of this book may be reproduced in any manner without prior written permission from the publisher. Write: Permissions, Wipf and Stock Publishers, 199 W. 8th Ave., Suite 3, Eugene, OR 97401.

Wipf & Stock
An Imprint of Wipf and Stock Publishers
199 W. 8th Ave., Suite 3
Eugene, OR 97401

www.wipfandstock.com

PAPERBACK ISBN: 979-8-3852-6039-3
HARDCOVER ISBN: 979-8-3852-6040-9
EBOOK ISBN: 979-8-3852-6041-6

VERSION NUMBER 11/21/25

Scripture quotations are from New Revised Standard Version Bible, copyright © 1989 National Council of the Churches of Christ in the United States of America. Used by permission. All rights reserved worldwide. All use of italics in Scripture quotations is added by the author.

Cover art "Field of Flowers." Created by Abby Coppock. Used with permission.

To the heart that ponders,
    Can Christianity be
    truly
        good?

Contents

Foreword by David Khalaf | ix
Preface | xv
Acknowledgments | xvii
An Introduction | xix

Part I. **A Bit on Good** | 1

Chapter 1. A Good Story About the Bible | 5
Chapter 2. A Good Bible Story | 18
Chapter 3. A Good Gospel Story | 32
Chapter 4. A Good Salvation Story | 45

Part II. **A Bit on Evolution** | 59

Chapter 5. An Evolutionary Atonement Story | 63
Chapter 6. An Evolutionary Afterlife Story | 81

Part III. **A Bit on Religious Tradition** | 109

Chapter 7. Held Together by Christian Life | 113

Bibliography | 121

Foreword

This book is about stories: the stories we grow up with, the messages we get from them, and the ways in which our lives are shaped by them—the ways in which *we* are shaped by them.

It makes sense, then, to introduce this book by way of a story: a story about a church in Portland, Oregon, that for years resembled all the other nondenominational churches in the United States. Founded with the intention to celebrate the goodness of the gospel in a newly developed neighborhood, Pearl Church was small but vibrant—a good place for most young families to raise their children, sharing with them the traditional messages of the Bible.

But as in all stories, there was a wrinkle. In this case, it was the fact that not *everybody* at Pearl was straight. As in many churches, these folks weren't just abstract notions described in newspapers; they were friends, neighbors, and family. They were *community*. They were loved. But they were second-class citizens. They lacked access to marriage, and they couldn't really be open about their sexuality outside of perhaps privately sharing their "struggles with same-sex attraction." To many at Pearl, this didn't seem right. No matter what their Christian upbringing may have taught them, they saw goodness in their friends and saw *no* goodness in excluding them. Their hearts and their heads were at odds.

FOREWORD

The wrinkle itched and irritated until one day it couldn't be ignored any longer. Those who were troubled by the issue began to look more critically at their faith. They wondered whether the good news they intended to bring to the city was, in fact, good. Others worried that the church was flirting with dangerous ideas that violated the sanctity of their beliefs. The board and pastors embarked upon a months-long process to examine the question of expanding the church's marriage practice to include same-sex couples. They read many books, had many conversations, and spent hours in prayer. They knew the decision would be fraught. They knew it would have grave consequences. They knew it could split the community. And the five members of the board knew it all would come down to a vote they would have to cast.

Let's pause here for a moment to understand what was going on. Essentially, the church was examining one particular story—the story of marriage—and trying to determine whether the messages and the lessons they had been taught about that story were valid and good. In today's traditional interpretation, Christian marriage is between one heterosexual woman and one heterosexual man. That, contemporary traditionalists believe, is the original design for marriage and the only acceptable telling of the marriage story. (Let's set aside for now the polygamy, concubines, and handmaids scattered throughout the pages of the Bible.)

Although this was an examination of marriage, really it was about much more. Stories don't exist in isolation. As you'll learn in this book, stories help set the table for a whole host of messages and beliefs about what is good and how we should live our lives. The conventional story of marriage, for example, comes bundled with a number of other beliefs, including but not limited to these below:

- The purpose of marriage is to procreate.
- Men are ordained to be the head of the household.
- Women have a subservient role in society.

- Marriage is a redemptive act that helps men and women keep each other on the path to salvation.

Reframing your understanding about one issue can cascade into something much larger: an entire examination of all of the stories you've been taught. Picking at the thread of one story can threaten to unravel the entire sweater. Welcome to deconstruction—it's both exhilarating and terrifying!

What are some of the threads of Christianity that you find yourself picking at? These are the stories that never quite sat right with you—the ones you believed only because you were told to believe them, or because you lacked a thoughtful and well-supported alternative. Mine are too numerous to count, but some were more prominent: Do nonbelievers really go to hell, a place of eternal torment? Were Adam and Eve real people or just archetypes—and what does that mean for the Bible's "infallibility"? Did Jesus really have to get sacrificed for our sins, and what does that act of violence say about the God we worship?

Some strains of Christianity today admonish this kind of deep examination because it threatens the dogma that maintains their authority. Others are open to examination but can't imagine that a story could be understood any way other than how they've heard it. That's not how it used to be, nor is it how it must be. As you'll discover in this book, reexamining the stories you've learned about Christianity is not only reasonable, but is an essential component to sustaining a flourishing faith. We can't call the gospel "living" and then expect stagnation; our understanding of the stories and lessons around Christianity can transform and evolve as we do, *because* we do.

This approach to faith is not counter to Christian traditions, but rather consistent with some of the most ancient practices. When you open yourself to reframing and re-understanding that which you assumed was immutable, you're participating in the same ancient tradition as some of the faith's greatest thinkers. That is my invitation to you as you delve into *Story and Table*: to approach the book with an open-heart longing for universally good news from a Divine Love.

Now let's return to our story. You may be wondering what became of Pearl Church. Three of the five board members voted to make space for LGBTQIA+ couples in the community. It was not an easy decision, and it was far from the end of the story. The other two members resigned and left the church. About half the congregation followed suit. Friendships were broken. Hurtful letters were circulated. Church finances suffered. For a time, it seemed like the church might not survive.

But out of that courageous act something beautiful grew. Those who stayed began to explore their faith more openly and honestly. They became less spiritually rigid, allowing their lives to be shaped by evolving understandings of sacred stories. They shared life together at a common table that, for the first time, was radically inclusive. And they became more awake to God, animated by Divine love that offered truly good news for all, not just some.

Today, Pearl Church is a thriving community. Its congregants have heard many of the ideas you are about to read. Pearl has been an incubator, wrestling with these new perspectives on ancient stories, testing their goodness, and demonstrating their practical application in lives lived out. It is a table that has created space for people to exist, heal, grow, and rejoice. It is a sanctuary where Christian life feels good and integrating.

On a personal note, I can speak to the many good ways in which Pearl and these stories have shaped my own life. My then-boyfriend (now husband), Constantin, and I began attending the church several months before the broadening of the marriage practice. As newer members, we weren't privy to all the conversations the leadership was having, but the following year we had the unique honor of being the first gay couple married at Pearl under the revised policy. Our wedding was officiated by the teaching pastor at Pearl, who is now our good friend and the author of this book, Mike Roth.

Story and Table is a book many of us have been longing for. This book is for you if you've seen the loose threads around modern Protestant Christianity but you've been wary of picking at them. This book is for you if you've found yourself questioning the goodness of your faith but you aren't ready to give up on it. This book is for you if you're looking for a nonviolent, anti-empire way forward that is both *new* and *ancient*—both *groundbreaking* and *grounded* in established traditions and coherent theology. Most of all, this book is for you if you're searching for a flourishing life that is animated by Divine Love.

So pull up a chair and join us at this table. We've been waiting for you.

David Khalaf
Co-author, *Modern Kinship: A Queer Guide to Christian Marriage*

Preface

This book proposes a reimagining of theology capable of sustaining truly good Christianity in the twenty-first century.

Biblical studies and church history situate the ideas proposed, although I imagine a good number of readers will experience them for the first time because they aren't often emphasized in modern-day Western Christianity.

It's truly unfortunate.

As this book demonstrates, the church has a beautiful tradition in which its theological expressions are shaped by evolving stages of human consciousness. Even so, many of today's theological iterations have been calcified by a Western fixation on dogma, which cannot account for today's context—socially, culturally, philosophically, or scientifically. The result is an irrelevant and increasingly dangerous Christianity insisting on violent, bigoted, and incoherent *truths*. To make matters worse, it's these very *truths* that a large majority of Christians today insist, "Believe or else!"

No, thank you.

A broad swath of pertinent and loving Christian thought exists for us to draw from and build on, and this book plumbs those depths. Ultimately, this book is an invitation. It's an invitation

PREFACE

into a deeply ancient and wonderfully evolving Christianity capable of holding our precious and singular lives in the ways and wisdom of Divine Love.

Acknowledgments

Jen, your attentive listening to soul-level knowing, insistence on asking the difficult questions, and audacity to follow the answers wherever they lead have encouraged our lifelong evolution. I'm grateful for the life we have made together, Pearl Church included. Thank you.

Pearl Church, Jesus said, "A tree is known by its fruit."[1] Your insatiable curiosity, spacious inclusion, and fidelity to the complexity and goodness of Divine Love are delicious. I'm inspired by the revolutionary way of Jesus you make manifest in this world. Thank you.

Mom, you were the first person to read me stories, tell me stories, and celebrate my own creation of stories. Because of you, I cherish storytelling. Thank you.

Dad, I still have the Bible you gave me at the height of my childhood nightmares. You told me to place it under my pillow to protect me while I sleep. I no longer believe in its magical powers, but its tales continue to inspire my life. Thank you.

Joseph, when everything falls apart you always show up. You hold my tears and terror in love. Thank you. And thank you for sharing with me in the journey of adulting and midlife.

---

1. Matt 12:33.

ACKNOWLEDGMENTS

Karl, through years of reading and discussing literature together you encourage my soul to sing. Thank you. And thank you for supporting my academic and creative dreams with your editorial craft.

Brett, you stood in front of my class with so much strength and vulnerability, vehemently shaking sheet metal to make the sound of thunder while passionately reading *Macbeth*. Since that day, I encounter art with an expectation to experience profundity that cracks my heart wide open. Thank you.

Marc, we were both in the midst of dying and rising—blurry-eyed, barely able to stand. That's when we began to meet and hug, so we wouldn't fall over. That's when somebody said, Pearl won't survive this. And you decided, yes it will. Thank you.

Ben, cultivating a sacred story and common table that animate life by Divine Love, with you, is a gift. Thank you.

Doreen, without your healing care and wisdom I wouldn't be who I am, where I am, or capable of sharing this book. Thank you.

An Introduction

Stories set the tables around which we live our lives. That's an important sentence. More than many of us realize.

Tables are the places—literally and metaphorically—around which we live our lives. For example, we spend a whole bunch of time around literal tables in homes, restaurants, cafeterias, bars, and parks, where we share in meals and conversations. But we spend even more time around metaphorical tables: occupational tables around which we work, create, produce, or manage; recreational tables around which we play; political tables around which we vote, march, and endlessly discuss; and for some, religious tables around which we gather, hope, and become.

So.
Many.
Tables.

Tables are the places around which we live our lives.

However, these tables don't just exist. They aren't *ex nihilo*—out of nothing. These tables are nurtured and shaped. Yes, nurtured and shaped by family systems, cultures, traditions, and personalities. And yet, undergirding every family system, culture, tradition, and personality are stories that give particular form to the tables we live around. For example, we have mealtime stories

AN INTRODUCTION

about gathering, eating, and connecting. We have occupational stories about what's necessary, meaningful, or a good fit for our lives. We have recreational stories about what's enjoyable and rejuvenating. We have political stories about what makes life together, work. And for some, we have religious stories about God, the Ground of our Being.

So.

Many.

Stories.

Stories are what give shape to the literal and metaphorical tables we spend our lives around.

Here's an example of the power of story. Growing up, I was told a story about the first Thanksgiving during which the pilgrims and indigenous peoples shared a meal together. This story made me feel really good about being a citizen of the United States, and it inspired gratitude on an annual basis. It was a pretty powerful story in my life until I began hearing and reading about other, more historical stories involving colonialism. And those stories made me feel sad, ashamed, and furious. Not surprisingly, those stories altered the literal Thanksgiving tables I gather around each year.

Here's another example of the power of story. When I was very young—probably four or five—my sweet Sunday school teacher used the flannelgraph to tell stories about God. If you know what the flannelgraph is, then we're probably religiously related, have the same Bible verses memorized, and can recall the motions to the song "Father Abraham Had Many Sons." For those of you who missed out on this particular medium of religious storytelling, the flannelgraph is a board covered in flannel that sits on an easel. The flannelgraph I remember was verdant green, and it filled every story with pastoral beauty. Paper cutouts of objects and people were able to stick on the flannelgraph, and they

AN INTRODUCTION

were moved around by our teacher as the Sunday school lesson unfolded. On the particular Sunday I have in mind, my sweet Sunday school teacher placed flames at the bottom of the flannelgraph and laid a couple of the pretend kids over the flames. She then went on to tell us a story about how we'd go into the flames forever if we didn't ask Jesus into our hearts.

That story deeply impacted the literal *and* metaphorical tables in my life. Over time, it became a lens through which I thought about God. It shaped my convictions about what was important. It caused me to worry, a lot, about friends and family members who didn't go to church. And I had many scary and sleepless nights as a result of that story.

Stories set the tables around which we live our lives.

For religious people—Christian people in particular—our stories about God and humans and the meaning of it all deeply impact our understanding of everything. For Christians, the influence of our religious stories extends out, well beyond religious tables, giving shape to every table.

Today, many Western, Protestant Christians are beginning to realize the significance of our Christian stories. As this awareness grows, we're becoming less willing than previous generations to accept incoherent "truths," dogma fostering violence, and faith animated by fear. As a result, troves of Christians are walking away from Christianity. And while I understand this response, it makes me wonder if a person can simply leave old stories behind?

In Plato's *Republic* we read these wise words about the power of stories:

> Anything that he receives into his mind at that age is likely to become indelible and unalterable; and therefore it is most

AN INTRODUCTION

important that the tales which the young first hear should be models of virtuous thoughts.[1]

If Plato is right then this is a real problem. Many of us were told tales that were not models of virtuous thought. Many of us were told tales that were incoherent, violent, and grounded in fear. Does this mean these tales are indelible and unalterable, especially for those of us who have been swimming in a particular pool of Christian stories for the majority of our lives?

Thankfully, no. We do have options.

One option is for a person to leave Christianity behind. To just walk away. That's a very sensible option. However, to be truly freed from the indelible and unalterable impact of religious stories, it will be important for those who walk away to intentionally formulate other stories—good stories—that, over time, begin to captivate imagination and replace the deep impressions made by the old Christian stories.[2] Today, some, even many, are beginning to do that important work.

Another option exists, though, and it gets at the soul of this book, *Story and Table*. This option invites us to critically rethink our Christian stories to ensure loving tables, around which Christians are freed and inspired to flourish.

This is the option I'm passionate about.

I have spent my entire life—personally, professionally, and academically—in Christian stories and at Christian tables. And like many others today, there came a point in my life when I thought I could no longer live my life as a Christian. I was beginning to pick up on the harm. I was beginning to notice the disintegration that

---

1. Plato, *Plato's Republic*, book 2 (Jowett, 45).
2. Neuroplasticity explains that our brains have the ability to form new neural pathways.

AN INTRODUCTION

my Christian story and table were causing in the world. I was beginning to feel more and more reticence about the idea of a perfect Bible, exclusion in Jesus' name, and Divine wrath. Because of this, I began to despise the violent and dominion aspects of the Christianity I was part of, and I nearly walked away. But then, there were graces. I would call them "Divine moments," during which my pursuit of becoming a theologian opened my mind to the vastness and richness of Christian thought well beyond the walls of Western, Protestant Christianity.

During this time, I became engrossed in the ancient and evolving meaning-making of Christian language—Story. At this same time, I was deep in the land of pastoring an eclectic, urban, highly educated, and inquisitive Christian community in downtown Portland—Table. Together, my studies as a theologian and my work as a pastor began to rub off on one another. I began to notice the deep connection between the stories we tell and the tables around which we live our lives. And in a moment—it was like being born again—I knew that I knew that I wanted to participate in undoing some of the sorrow by expressing an ancient, evolving, and truly good way of being Christian, today.

With this context in mind, this book sets a foundation for good stories that set loving tables by exploring core Christian theologies. These theologies include the Bible, the gospel, salvation, atonement, and the afterlife.

The chapters in this book progress simply and similarly:

- Summary of a religious story many Western, Protestant Christians have been told.
- Observations on the kind of table this religious story sets.
- Summary of another religious story, which many Western, Protestant Christians have not been told.
- Observations on the kind of table this religious story sets.

Part I. A Bit on Good

In the beginning, the book of Genesis explains that God created.[1]

God created light.
> God created sky.
>> God created water, land, and vegetation.
>>> God created sun and moon.
>>>> God created creatures.
>>>>> God created humans.

About that which God created, Genesis tells us it was assessed and found by God to be good.

Good.

It's a word often used when referring to the creation account, but I don't think it's garnered the appreciation it deserves. Genesis explains each step in the creation process concluded with the determination of good. In other words, the creation was assessed, considered, and evaluated for its *goodness*. This determination was so important that it concludes the creation account in Genesis, "God saw everything . . . made, and indeed, it was very good."[2]

---

1. Gen 1:1–31.
2. Gen 1:31a.

PART I. A BIT ON GOOD

This seems important. The determining factor for that which God created was the inherent goodness of that which was created.

In Hebrew, the primary word translated as "good" is *tov*. The standard definition for *tov* is "to be good in all respects," and it's described by a handful of adjectives:

> *Tov* is joyful and glad.
> *Tov* is pleasant, sweet, and fair.
> *Tov* is advisable.
> *Tov* is appropriate and becoming.
> *Tov* is valuable.[3]

Isn't that beautiful?

God created and that which God created was assessed and determined to be good—joyful, glad, pleasant, sweet, fair, advisable, appropriate, becoming, and valuable—in all respects.

I believe this process of discernment can assist us in our Christian lives. For if the notion of good was the determining factor for God in the creation account, then it's reasonable to conclude that the creation of Christian life should be, similarly, good. Therefore, let's pause to thoughtfully ask some questions:

> Is our dogma good?
> Is our doctrine good?
> Is our theology good?
> Is our Christian life good?

Many Christians today ignore these evaluative questions by declaring that these expressions are "historical" or "biblical." However,

---

3. *HALOT*, s.v. "טוֹב" (throughout, *HALOT* refers to Baumgartner and Koehler, *Hebrew and Aramaic Lexicon of the Old Testament*).

PART I. A BIT ON GOOD

doing so is fraught with a top-down mentality demanding unquestionable acquiescence. It makes me want to ask, why? Why isn't the goodness of our Christian expressions a determining factor for living Christian life? Why must we resort to other determining factors when that which is good is so wonderfully *good*?

Besides the use of good to affirm creation is the presence of Jesus' good gospel.[4] The word "gospel" derives from the Greek word *euaggelion*, which can also be translated as "good news."[5] This is the word the biblical authors use throughout their writings to name Jesus' message—*euaggelion*, gospel, good news. But there's more good to be had. After proclaiming his good news in the synagogue, we read, "All spoke well of [Jesus] and were amazed at the gracious words that came from his mouth."[6] They were *amazed* by his *gracious* words.

Let's not miss the theme here. In the Genesis account, God assessed and determined the creation was good. Throughout the Gospels, the biblical authors used "good news" as the paradigmatic expression to name that which Jesus proclaimed. And after Jesus proclaimed this good news in the synagogue, the audience was amazed by his gracious words.

Good.
Good.
Good.

That's what God is said to create—good. And that's what Jesus' gospel is—good. So good that Jesus' audience was amazed over and over again.

---

4. Luke 4:16–19.
5. εὐαγγέλιον can be translated as "good news" or "gospel" (BDAG, s.v. "εὐαγγέλιον"; throughout, BDAG refers to Bauer, Danker, Arndt, and Gingrich's *Greek-English Lexicon of the New Testament*).
6. Luke 4:22a.

3

PART I. A BIT ON GOOD

It's to this ancient goodness we now turn. The following chapters explore that which is good in some of our Christian expressions. In particular, the following four chapters explore our good Bible, good gospel, and good salvation. My sincere hope is that we—like Jesus' original audience—will be wooed by goodness into Christian life that is truly and wonderfully good.

Chapter 1. A Good Story About the Bible

This chapter explores stories told about the Bible. The consequences of these stories cannot be minimized. They fundamentally shape a person's reading and understanding of everything in the Bible.

The Story We Have Been Told

For many of us, the story told about the Bible goes like this:

> God—who is perfect—inspired the Bible's writings. Therefore, the writings contained within the Bible are infallible and inerrant.

Infallible means the Bible is incapable of making mistakes.

Inerrant means the Bible is incapable of being wrong.

The Table This Story Sets

Let's now consider some of the implications that this particular story about the Bible has on the lives of people.

Imagine for a moment that you pick up your Bible and begin to read the book of Genesis. In chapter 1, verse 7, you come across

PART I. A BIT ON GOOD

these words about the creation: "So God made the dome." The Hebrew word for "dome" is *raqia*, which refers to a beaten metal plate, a firmament, a solid vault up in the sky.[1] However, living as a person in the twenty-first century, you know there isn't a solid vault up in the sky. Spacecrafts filled with astronauts go straight into space without needing to break through any kind of solid material.

That's a cosmological problem in the Bible.

Now, imagine you're doing some research on that betrayer, Judas Iscariot. You read in Matt 27 that he died by suicide—by hanging, to be specific. But then you read in Acts 1 that Judas didn't actually die by suicide. Instead, you read that Judas fell over, burst open, and his bowels gushed out.

That's a historical problem in the Bible.

Finally, imagine you read these words in Deut 20:

> But as for the towns of these peoples that the LORD your God is giving you as an inheritance, you must not let anything that breathes remain alive. You shall annihilate them—the Hittites and the Amorites, the Canaanites and the Perizzites, the Hivites and the Jebusites—just as the LORD your God has commanded.[2]

But then, you flip over to Matt 5 and read these words:

> You have heard that it was said, "You shall love your neighbor and hate your enemy." But I say to you, love your enemies and pray for those who persecute you, so that you may be children of your Father in Heaven; for

---

1. The beaten metal plate, or bow; firmament, the firm vault of heaven (*HALOT*, s.v. "רָקִיעַ"); Septuagint, στερέωμα; Vulgate, *firmamentum*.
2. Deut 20:16–17.

CHAPTER 1. A GOOD STORY ABOUT THE BIBLE

he makes his sun rise on the evil and on the good, and sends rain on the righteous and on the unrighteous.[3]

That's a theological problem in the Bible.

Question: What are we to do with these cosmological, historical, and theological problems?

If you believe in a story about the Bible insisting on the Bible's perfection, then you're forced to try and harmonize any of its apparent problems. This word "harmonize" is crucial. The work of harmonization is grounded in a story about a perfect Bible, without error, because it's the very word of God. Therefore, any and all apparent problems—whether they be cosmological or historical or theological—are not truly problems. According to this particular story about the Bible, either our cosmology or our history or our theological understanding must be wrong, and to take this perfect text seriously, a person must harmonize any apparent problems.

Let's tease this out.

Using God's directive to annihilate every person in the land, harmonization attempts reason to make sense of this problematic text. The reason goes something like this:

> God is sovereign and could have created these people for the sole purpose of destroying them. Therefore, God's judgment is providential.
>
> Or, God knows all things, and so God knew the people in the land would never come to salvation. Therefore, God's judgment is just.
>
> Or, God takes holiness seriously, and God didn't want Israel to be tempted and to stray into idolatry and sin. Therefore, God's judgment is loving.

3. Matt 5:43–45.

PART I. A BIT ON GOOD

At times, even those who believe in a story about a perfect Bible find this kind of reasoning unhelpful. Unfortunately, rather than considering a different story about the Bible, they double down with explanations such as these:

> "I don't care if a particular text is violent or unreasonable."
>
> "I don't care if a particular text is in conflict with cosmological or historical findings."
>
> "I don't care if a particular text is contradicted by other texts in the Bible."
>
> "God said it, I believe it."

Notice the kind of table that's set by this story about a perfect Bible.

> *One feature is people are forced to try and make sense of the Bible's problems by using strange logic, which is actually more like contortion than rational thought.*

Wouldn't you agree?

God created people for the purpose of killing them?

God knew some people wouldn't change, and so God had them massacred?

God wanted to protect the holiness of Israel, and so God commanded the annihilation of entire people groups?

No. This "reasoning" only makes sense to those who believe in a story about a perfect Bible. Tragically, such belief sets a table around which Divine violence is justifiable and, at times, enacted today.

> *A second feature of the table this story about the Bible sets is an insistence that God is violent, which is okay, and quite possibly necessary.*

CHAPTER 1. A GOOD STORY ABOUT THE BIBLE

The potentiality for harm caused by this interpretive solution to biblical problems is incalculable. To insist on "God said it, I believe it" despite a text's violence, lack of reason, conflict with cosmological or historical findings, or clear contradiction with other texts, is to insist on appreciating—and quite possibly appropriating—violent, racist, misogynistic, homophobic, etc. ideologies.

In extended conversations with people who hold to this story about the Bible, I have been told more than once, "I'm as uncomfortable with these texts as you are." Or, "I don't like this any more than you do." Or, "If it weren't in the Bible, then I'd think differently." Yet, all of these concerns are ignored with the quip "But God said it, so I believe it."

Herein lies a significant question: Did God say it? Many Christians today say *yes*. The reason they say *yes* is because they believe in a particular story about the Bible, which is this: God—who is perfect—inspired the Bible's writings. Therefore, the writings contained within the Bible are infallible and inerrant.

The Story We Need to Hear

The words "infallible" and "inerrant" do not exist in the Bible. These are extrabiblical words; these are extrabiblical concepts being applied to the Bible.

Consider these interesting words, by the great C. S. Lewis, about God's command to annihilate entire people groups:

> On my view one must apply something of the same sort of explanation to, say, the atrocities (and treacheries) of Joshua. I see the grave danger we run by doing so; but the dangers of believing in a God whom we cannot but regard as evil, and then, in mere terrified flattery calling Him "good" and worshiping Him, is still greater danger. The ultimate question is whether

PART I. A BIT ON GOOD

the doctrine of the goodness of God or that of the inerrancy of Scripture is to prevail when they conflict. I think the doctrine of the goodness of God is the more certain of the two.[4]

With these brief words, Lewis argues for that which many Christians today would call "heresy." He not only questions the doctrine of inerrancy but he denounces it because he cannot comprehend calling God "good," and worshiping God, if God told Israel to commit genocide.

Lewis's ability to critique the biblical idea of a God who commands genocide brings us to a different story about the Bible, which goes like this:

> The Bible—albeit sacred and inspired by God—was written by humans.

This perspective on the Bible goes beyond Lewis. Consider these words about the Bible by esteemed Christian theologians:[5]

Augustine in his book *On Christian Doctrine*:

> Whatever there is in the word of God that cannot, when taken literally, be referred either to purity of life or soundness of doctrine, you may set down as figurative.[6]

---

4. Lewis, *Narnia, Cambridge, and Joy*, 1512.

5. I'm indebted to Stephen D. Benin and his book *The Footprints of God: Divine Accommodation in Jewish and Christian Thought* and Kenton L. Sparks's *Sacred Word Broken Word: Biblical Authority and the Dark Side of Scripture* for pointing me toward historical perspectives and writings on the Bible as an inspired text written by humans.

6. Augustine, *On Christian Doctrine* 3.10.14 (*NPNF* 2:560); throughout, *NPNF* refers to the *Nicene and Post-Nicene Fathers*, and the attached number indicates whether the first or second series.

CHAPTER 1. A GOOD STORY ABOUT THE BIBLE

Gregory the Great in his work *Morals on the Book of Job*:

> Yet doubtless whereas the literal words when set against each other cannot be made to agree, they point out some other meaning in themselves which we are to seek for.[7]

John Wesley in *The Works of John Wesley*:

> This is true, if the literal sense of these Scriptures were absurd, and apparently contrary to reason, then we should be obliged not to interpret them according to the letter, but to look out for a looser meaning.[8]

Karl Barth in *Church Dogmatics*:

> Not only part but all that they say [in the Bible] is historically related and conditioned.[9]

Dietrich Bonhoeffer in his *Reflections on the Bible*:

> We must read this book of books with all human methods. But through the fragile and broken Bible, God meets us in the voice of the Risen One.[10]

A few key points:

> The Bible is the book of books, yet it is fragile and broken (Bonhoeffer).
>
> Contradictory and absurd texts should be understood in some other way than literal (Augustine, Gregory the Great, Wesley).

---

7. Gregory the Great, *Morals on the Book of Job* 1.1.3 (Parker et al., 1:7).
8. Wesley, *Sermons IV*, 337.
9. Barth, *Church Dogmatics*, 1/2:509.
10. Bonhoeffer, *Reflections on the Bible*, 15.

PART I. A BIT ON GOOD

> The Bible cannot escape the consciousness within which it was written (Barth).

Clearly, these giants in Christianity were able to write about the Bible in these ways because they existed within a different story about the Bible. For them, the Bible wasn't infallible; it was fallible. For them, the Bible wasn't inerrant; it was errant. For although it was inspired by God, it was understood to be penned by humans. And so, when they came across cosmological, historical, or theological problems in the Bible, they weren't forced to harmonize. Instead, they were able to accommodate.

The notion of accommodation is grounded in an understanding that the Bible—albeit sacred and inspired—was written by humans. As a result of this understanding, "accommodations" are able to be made for the spiritual and intellectual limitations of the Bible's human authors.

This changes everything.

The Table This Story Sets

Returning to mass genocide in God's name, we're no longer forced into strange logic or checking reason at the door.

A feature of the table this story about the Bible sets includes both logic and reason.

Did God tell Israel to commit genocide? Of course not. Every ancient people went to war believing their god told them to. When they won, they believed their god was on their side; when they lost, they believed their god was against them. That's how ancient people thought.[11]

---

11. A classic example of how ancient people believed God was either for them or against them, based on the outcome of war, is located in Josh 7. In this story, Israel believes God caused them to lose a battle against the people living in Ai because Achan hid spoil in his tent. After Achan's confession, Israel

CHAPTER 1. A GOOD STORY ABOUT THE BIBLE

Freed by accommodation to bring our logic and reason to the Bible, we're no longer compelled to believe God is pro-genocide. Nor are we pressured to take strange steps to defend Divine violence or any other harmful text. Much the opposite, in fact. Through accommodation, a passage like Deut 20 can result in helpful human warning:

> We humans have a tendency to use violence to get what we want and to procure our own safety.
>
> More so, we humans have a tendency to believe God is not only okay with our violence but commissions our violence.
>
> More so, we humans have a tendency to act violently because we think God is for us and against them.

Freed from a literal interpretation at every turn because "God said it," the Bible becomes an invitation to explore what ancient people had to say about life and God. Through this understanding, accommodation sets us to wrestling with the Bible, with sensitivity to human consciousness, to discern goodness, love, and wisdom for today.

A second feature of the table this story about the Bible sets is discerning good.

Depending on the text, the lessons are many. For example, a text could

> warn us of old human biases,
>
> enliven us by surprising moments of kindness,
>
> repulse us by bigotry,
>
> or, open us to human encounters with Divine Love.

---

stoned him to death and then routed Ai in a second battle. This result confirmed their belief in God being, once again, on their side.

Through accommodation, we're able to use all of our interpretive tools to thoughtfully learn from this ancient and sacred collection of writings we Christians call "the Bible."

Biblical Authority

If you grew up in the first story about the Bible I told, then you may be feeling a bit unsettled regarding the Bible's authority. This is because—in the first story about the Bible—its authority is the result of it being God's perfect word. However, as previously explained, this becomes problematic when we encounter cosmological, historical, or theological problems in the Bible. The good news is another reason for the Bible's authority exists, which is, the Bible's formation.

Buckle up. I'm going to give a ten-thousand-foot overview of the Bible's formation to explain its authority.[12]

The Bible was written by many different authors and editors.

The oldest writings in the Hebrew Scriptures are from the eighth century BCE.

The newest writings in the Hebrew Scriptures are from the second century BCE.

The oldest writings in the New Testament are from 50 CE.

The newest writings in the New Testament are from around 120 CE.

With this information, the creation of the books in the Bible span about nine hundred years.

---

12. For this overview, I'm indebted to Paget and Schaper, *Beginnings to 600*; Barton, *History of the Bible*; Childs, *Old Testament as Scripture*; Borg, *Evolution of the Word*; Ehrman, *Bible*; Kugel, *Bible as It Was*; and Chilton et al., *Cambridge Companion to the Bible*.

CHAPTER 1. A GOOD STORY ABOUT THE BIBLE

Think about that. These books were being written over an almost one-thousand-year period dating back to between 1,900 and 2,800 years ago. The United States is only 250 years old. Consider how much thought and behavior have changed in that brief time period. With this in mind, the Bible's authors existed in various cultures, social mores, and stages of human consciousness.

The Bible was written in three different languages—Hebrew, Aramaic, and Greek.

The Bible contains different types, genres, and forms of literature.

And the books of the Bible became books in the Bible through a messy, overlapping, threefold process, which looked like this:

> First, the books were written.
>
> Second, a book became sacred.[13]
>
>> That's to say, many books were written but the books that ended up in the Bible—over time—became known as special books, elevated books, sacred books in the life of Israel and the church.
>
> Third, a book became fixed as canon.
>
>> That's to say, a book became a book in the Bible.

Now, here's what's wild about the books that became books in the Bible. God did not bellow from heaven, "These are the books of the Bible." Nor was there a council held or a group of leaders who ruled on canonization.[14] Instead, through the messy, threefold process

---

13. The more accurate word for books that made it to this second phase is "scripture." However, because Christians today think of "scripture" as the books that are in the Bible, I'm using the word "sacred" to describe the books that were elevated above common books in this second phase. Of course, every book in the Bible made it to this phase, but there were books that never made it out of this phase. For example, 1 Enoch and the gnostic Gospels.

14. In academically rigorous historical overviews of the Council of Nicaea—e.g., Kim's *Cambridge Companion to the Council of Nicaea*—no mention

just explained, the books were written, eventually became sacred, until finally, they were fixed as books in the Bible.

Biblical scholars suggest the books in the Hebrew Scriptures acquired an official status for Jews by the end of the first century CE, which was about two hundred years after the last book was written. Biblical scholars suggest the books in the New Testament acquired an official status by the fourth century CE, which was, also, about two hundred years after the last book was written.[15]

How is this information helpful in relation to the Bible's authority? Well, in the first story I told, the Bible's authority rose from being God's perfect word: "God said it, I believe it." But that makes me want to ask, is that authority? That kind of authority reminds me of when I was young and my parents told me something. I just accepted what they said. However, as I grew and entered adolescence, when my parents told me something I often needed more information and would sometimes ask, "Why?" And when they responded by saying, "Because I said so" their words actually lost authority. Not because I was rebellious but because I was growing.

The word "authority" refers to power that influences. And as I grew, "Because I said so" lost the power to influence as assumed authority was eclipsed by my developmental need for earned authority.

This brings me to why I spent time telling you about how the Bible became the Bible.

---

of a decision exists regarding which books belong in the Bible. Supporting this point is biblical scholar John Barton, who explains, "The idea that books other than those now in the New Testament should be positively excluded [was] a process that was not complete until the late fourth century." *History of the Bible*, 263.

15. Some evidence exists supporting the idea that the New Testament books began to be seen less and less as informal documents and more and more like fixed canon by late second century CE. However, "the oldest surviving document in which exactly the present New Testament books are listed... is found in Athanasius' *Festal Letter of 367CE*." Barton, *History of the Bible*, 265.

CHAPTER 1. A GOOD STORY ABOUT THE BIBLE

A third feature of the table this story about the Bible sets is earned authority.

Ancient books written over a nearly one-thousand-year period?

Two two-hundred-year periods during which certain books rose to prominence as "sacred" until, eventually, entire communities—Jewish and Christian—declared, "These are biblical"?

That's one of the longest book formation processes in human history.

Today, we experience quite the opposite, don't we? Today, we're inundated by ever-increasing texts, tweets, posts, articles, magazines, and books—often, with very little standardization for quality or editorial process. Standing in stark contrast to these expedient mediums of written communication is the ancient, prolonged, and communal process of the Bible's formation, which I believe stands out as worthy of influence. That's to say, it bears the weight of earned authority. Not because "God said it, so I believe it." Rather, because God inspired it, humans wrote it, and over a very long period of time, entire communities—Jewish and Christian—chose to esteem it. Very few books in the world bear the weight of this kind of authority. And we modern humans get to hold this ancient, messy, and inspired book in our laps as we use all of our tools for discerning its wisdom and goodness for our lives and world, today.

Chapter 2. A Good Bible Story

In the previous chapter, I addressed stories told about the Bible. In this chapter, I address the story in the Bible.

The Story We Have Been Told

The Bible tells a story that begins in Genesis, rises throughout the Hebrew Scriptures and New Testament, and concludes in Revelation. With this in mind, the Bible has a narrative arc, which is called a "plot." A plot has five movements:

First, background.

Second, an inciting incident, which makes the story go.

Third, many layers of rising action.

Fourth, the crescendo, called "climax."

And fifth, the denouement; the conclusion—the end.

The most important part of a story is its inciting incident, also known as the problem. This is because by the time we get to the climax of a story, the problem is either resolved, which makes the story a comedy, or the problem remains unresolved—maybe even exacerbated—which makes the story a tragedy. This means the inciting incident and the climax are intrinsically connected when it comes to interpreting the meaning of a story.

CHAPTER 2. A GOOD BIBLE STORY

With this understanding of plot, the Bible story's inciting incident is located in Gen 3. In this chapter, Adam and Eve eat from a tree God told them to avoid. The tree has a name, "the knowledge of good and evil." After eating from the tree of the knowledge of good and evil, Adam and Eve are filled with guilt and shame. As a result, they cover themselves with leaves, and when they hear God out on an evening walk in the garden they hide behind the trees. Cursed, God sends them away—east of Eden—to live out their lives in this world we humans call "home."

That's the inciting incident.

I'll now explain the interpretation of the inciting incident held by many people today. This interpretation actually has a name, which is "original sin." According to the interpretation of original sin, Adam and Eve's disobedience abruptly and catastrophically altered the world, and human beings became inherently depraved.

Let's now skip ahead to the Bible story's climax, which is located near the end of all four Gospels.[1] The Bible story's climax occurs when Jesus, the Son of God, is crucified on a cross, which is sometimes called a "tree."[2]

> On this tree,
> > Jesus' body is broken,
> > his blood is poured out.
> Three days later,
> > he is resurrected to new life.

---

1. Some scholars may suggest the climax is at the end of the book of Revelation, but I'm intentionally choosing the end of the Gospels for two reasons. First, Jesus' death and resurrection are the climactic, literary focus of the New Testament, proven by four Gospels that all tell this part of Jesus' story. Second, whether the climax is Jesus' death and resurrection or closer to the end of Revelation, the interpretive points I highlight do not change.

2. Acts 5:30.

PART I. A BIT ON GOOD

I'll now explain the interpretation of the climax held by many people today. Anyone who believes in Jesus' death on a cross and shed blood for the forgiveness of their sins is made new. No longer a child of Adam and Eve but a child of God, their citizenship is transferred from this world and an eternity in hell to a heavenly kingdom and an eternity in bliss.

With all of this in mind, I'd like to invite you to consider an important question: Is today's common interpretation of the Bible story's inciting incident and climax a comedy or a tragedy? Well, according to the interpretation of original sin, Adam and Eve's disobedience abruptly and catastrophically altered the world. However, in the climax of this story, the world doesn't immediately change back into something like Eden.

That's not good, is it?

Furthermore, according to the interpretation of original sin, all human beings became immediately depraved due to something somebody else—Adam and Eve—did. However, in the climax of this story, when Jesus dies and rises, the curse of Adam and Eve is not immediately reversed. That's to say, nobody becomes immediately blameless. Far from it, in fact. According to today's common interpretation, only those who choose to believe in Jesus' shed blood for the forgiveness of their sins become children of God with the hope of heaven.

That's not good either, is it?

At best, this interpretation of the Bible story is a comedy for the few who believe. However, for the rest of humankind, this interpretation is a horrifying tragedy because the majority of humans in this world remain depraved and destined to a place of eternal torment in hell. Adding to this sorrow is the realization that Jesus is less powerful than Adam and Eve because he's unable to immediately and fully reverse the damage they caused.

CHAPTER 2. A GOOD BIBLE STORY

The Table This Story Sets

Before sharing a more coherent interpretation of the Bible story's inciting incident and climax, I want to explore the kind of table this particular interpretation sets in the lives of people.

One feature of the table this interpretation of the Bible story sets is transactional faith.

Believe these things, then you are saved, and you'll end up in heaven forever. It's this emphasis on momentary belief that then becomes the most important moment of the human experience. But what about the rest of our human experiences? What bearing does this Bible story have on our lives outside of accepting this one thing? It makes me want to ask, is faith nothing more than one momentary transaction?

A second feature of the table this interpretation of the Bible story sets is a diminishing of the Bible.

Reading the Bible through the lens of original sin makes little sense of Gen 4, all the way up to the point in each Gospel when Jesus is crucified, buried, and resurrected. What then is the purpose of the stories, poems, prayers, and prophetic messages between Gen 4 and Jesus' crucifixion? What about Abraham, the exodus out of Egypt, the wandering in the wilderness, life in the promised land, messages from the prophets, and exile in Babylon? According to this particular interpretation of the Bible story, those large swaths of Scripture are pretty much unnecessary; they don't significantly affect the story.

It's the same for Jesus' life. According to this particular interpretation of the Bible story—other than, perhaps, Jesus' miraculous birth—Jesus' life and ministry have little bearing on resolving the inciting incident's problem. What then is the purpose of Jesus' sermons, teachings, interactions, and miracles?

PART I. A BIT ON GOOD

> *A third feature of the table this interpretation of*
> *the Bible story sets is a calamitous insistence*
> *on the depravity of humans.*

Countless times, I have heard parents who live within this particular interpretation of the Bible story state—when their toddler or elementary kid or adolescent is spunky or pushing boundaries or questioning authority—something like, "There, there it is. That depravity, that fallenness!"

Of course, there could be another way to interpret a child's spunk or boundary pushing or questions:

> They're growing.
>
> They're developing.
>
> They're doing the important work of individuating, finding their own voice, and learning in ways that make sense to them.

Isn't this true for us all?

Unfortunately, many who grew up reading the Bible through the lens of original sin are inclined to believe the worst about themselves and others. As a result, they're inclined to doubt goodness in themselves and others.

It's a calamitous world.

And this calamitous world absolutely dismantles the notion of rehabilitation—because how is any person capable of making change or healing or growing up into wisdom and goodness if they are truly and inherently depraved? That would be utterly hopeless, wouldn't it?

> *A fourth feature of the table this interpretation of*
> *the Bible story sets is really bad news.*

CHAPTER 2. A GOOD BIBLE STORY

If Jesus is the solution to the problem Adam and Eve caused, then he is an impotent solution because he doesn't immediately and fully resolve that which Adam and Eve broke. More so, the solution is inequitable because some people will never get to hear this particular interpretation of the Bible story, so they won't even have a chance to believe the right things. Furthermore, there will be many countless others who do hear about this particular interpretation but it won't make sense to them, or for one reason or another they won't believe it. This means the majority of humans throughout human history are going to a place of eternal torment forever, while only a select few end up in heaven.

No, thank you.

That's a terrible story.

It's a violent story.

It's a story rotten at the core with tragedy.

The Story We Need to Hear

The words "original sin" were coined by Augustine, who was working off of a Latin translation of Rom 5:12, which led him to believe all sinned in Adam.[3] However, the Greek text explains, "because all have sinned," indicating we all sin in the way of Adam, rather than indicating we all sinned in Adam.[4]

This interpretive distinction must not be understated.

In the former, inaccurate interpretation, we are all depraved at conception. However, in the latter, more accurate interpretation, Adam is a typology for humankind—which is to say, "We all, like

---

3. Augustine, *City of God* 13.13 (NPNF 2:251); Walton, *Lost World of Adam and Eve*, proposition 17, 153–60.
4. Moo, *Epistle to Romans*, 314–50; Dunn, *Romans 1–8*, 271–74.

PART I. A BIT ON GOOD

Adam, sin." This is the meaning adopted by most commentators today, which means Rom 5:12 is actually about the way in which we all sin, like Adam.[5] And how do we all do that?

That's a great question.

We're now ready for a different interpretation of the Bible story's inciting incident and climax. It's an interpretation I have found

---

5. Moo, *Epistle to the Romans*, 321. Besides Augustine's mistranslation of Rom 5:12, the theory of original sin is deeply problematic. Here are some of the primary reasons: First, the words "original sin" don't exist anywhere in the Bible. Second, Judaism doesn't have a concept of original sin. This makes good sense because, third, following Gen 3, Adam and Eve's "fall" isn't mentioned in the Hebrew Scriptures. Outside of being mentioned as the parents of Cain, Abel, and Seth in Gen 5 and Adam being named in a genealogy in 1 Chr 1, they aren't mentioned, which should be shocking. If Adam and Eve depraved every human and cataclysmically altered the world, the Hebrew Scriptures should say something about that, right? Fourth, according to Augustine's theory of original sin, Adam's "guilty nature" is transmitted through sexual union to Adam and Eve's offspring. Augustine, *City of God* 13.2 (*NPNF* 2:246). Based on this theory, some thoughtful questions must be asked, such as, Can a guilty nature really be passed on through sexual union? Do semen and an egg carry the weight of spiritual guilt? In my mind, the obvious answer to these questions is no. Augustine was fashioning theology based on archaic and erroneous biological insights. Continuing with science, many scholars don't think there was an actual Adam and Eve. But for a moment, let's say they existed. Were Adam and Eve the progenitors of *every* human being? And if not, what about the humans who didn't come from Adam and Eve? Did their sexual union pass on spiritual guilt? And if so, *how*, since these other human beings weren't in the hereditary line of Adam and Eve? Fifth, the theory of original sin is the result of a genre classification problem. If the story of Gen 1–3 is to be read literally and understood scientifically, then these chapters are deeply problematic. For example, there is no firmament in the sky (Gen 1:6–7), there could be no day and night on day 1 of creation (Gen 1:3–5) if the sun, moon, and stars weren't created until day 4 (Gen 1:14–19), and clearly, the world was not created in seven literal days. Also, if we're reading the text honestly, snakes do not talk and trees do not contain fruit that when eaten alter the state of every created thing. For reasons like these, many scholars today read Gen 1–3 as "functional origins." Functional origin stories focus on order and function rather than literal materiality. And so, the creation and "fall" stories are not *literally* explaining what happened in the earliest days of our world. Rather, they are *literally* explaining meaning, i.e., God is generative, creative, personal, etc.; God invites humankind into creative work, etc.

CHAPTER 2. A GOOD BIBLE STORY

to be literarily coherent and unequivocally beneficial for human flourishing—in other words, a really good story.

Prior to Augustine's coining of original sin was the notion that humans are tasked with growing up from infancy into adulthood. About this process of growth, third-century church father Irenaeus explains,

> For as it certainly is in the power of a mother to give strong food to her infant but she does not do so, as the child is not yet able to receive more substantial nourishment; so also it was possible for God Himself to have made man perfect from the first, but man could not receive this perfection, being as yet an infant.[6]

According to Irenaeus, because it is physiologically impossible for humans to immediately grow up, we must begin—like all living things—at the beginning. However, as Gen 3 explains, Adam and Eve weren't okay with that. They wanted perfect knowledge, like God's, thereby attempting what can be called "wisdom grasping," by eating the fruit.

About the fruit Adam and Eve ate, consider these words from second-century apologist Theophilus of Antioch:

> For there was nothing else in the fruit than only knowledge; but knowledge is good when one uses it discreetly. But Adam being yet an infant in age, was on this account as yet unable to receive knowledge worthily. For now, also, when a child is born it is not at once able to eat bread, but is nourished first with milk, and then, with the increment of years, it advances to solid food. . . . Besides, it is unseemly that children in infancy be

---

6. Irenaeus, *Against Heresies* 3.38.1 (*ANF* 1:521); throughout, *ANF* refers to the *Ante-Nicene Fathers*.

PART I. A BIT ON GOOD

wise beyond their years; for as in stature one increases in an orderly progress, so also in wisdom.[7]

Isn't that beautiful?

And human?

Yes!

Based on this perspective, the Divine invitation was for Adam and Eve to grow up into wisdom and knowledge in the only way possible: in an orderly progress. However, Adam and Eve were unwilling to surrender to the natural process for progress. They attempted to gain perfect knowledge without going on the human journey of growing up. As a result, they came to know shame, guilt, and the experience of distance from the Divine—something we all experience when we fall short of our own expectations for perfection, now.

Based on this interpretation of the inciting incident, let's consider the climax. In contrast to Adam and Eve's wisdom grasping is Jesus, who—as exemplar—is filled with Spirit, grows in strength and wisdom, and exhibits a life marked by the fullness of love.[8] Ultimately, we observe Jesus subverting the Adam-story when he is crucified on a cross—sometimes called a "tree"—and three days later is raised to new life, inviting, "Follow after me."[9]

> Follow after me.
> Into life, death, and resurrection—
>> the only way
>> to grow up

---

7. Theophilus, *Theophilus to Autolycus* 2.25 (*ANF* 2:104).

8. Filled with Spirit (Luke 1:15); grows in strength and wisdom (Luke 2:40).

9. Acts 5:30 refers to the cross as a tree. After resurrecting, Jesus invites, "Follow me" (John 21:19).

> into the strength and wisdom,
> of love.

The Table This Story Sets

We're now ready to consider the features of a table set by this interpretation of the Bible story's inciting incident and climax.

> *One feature is incredible hope.*

Adam and Eve did not cataclysmically alter humankind and the creation. Rather, they are simply an example of humankind's "wisdom grasping" to become like God without living life.

This is good news.

You are not inherently depraved. You are wonderfully glorious and full of potential. Yet, we humans do have a proclivity toward perfection now, don't we?

> *A second feature of the table this interpretation of the Bible story sets is Divine patience.*

In Genesis, it isn't God who impatiently desires Adam and Eve to grow up as fast as possible. That was Adam and Eve's desire, remember? It was God who graciously and lovingly commanded, "Do not eat from the tree of knowledge of good and evil." This interpretation of the Bible story sets a table that encourages patience.

> Patience with our own lives.
> Patience with the lives of others.
> Patience with the development of humankind.

Wholeness and goodness take time to grow up into. Mistakes must be made, lessons must be learned, and this is the Divine invitation:

PART I. A BIT ON GOOD

to live out our lives on this earth while we grow—individually and as a species—into ever more goodness, wisdom, and ultimately, love. For truly, is there any other path to progress?

> *A third feature of the table this interpretation of the Bible story sets is encouraging progress.*

According to this understanding of the Bible story, everything in the Bible matters. By reading it from beginning to end, we're able to observe—albeit slowly—progress. For example, in the Bible we're able to notice an encouraging progression from an emphasis on law, to an emphasis on love; from an insistence on obedience, to an insistence on grace; from a focus on differences that separate, to a focus on similarities that encourage union; from a beginning in chaos, to an ending in peace.[10]

Of course, the latest books in the Bible were written in the second century CE, and so the full expressions of love, grace, and peace don't reach culmination in the Bible. However, the Bible bears witness to humankind's progress. It demonstrates that growth is possible. And it beckons us ever forward, until love is made fully manifest.[11]

---

10. Law (Exod 20:1–17) to love (Matt 5:38–39, 43–45); obedience (Deut 27–28) to grace (Rom 3–8); differences (Gen 28) to similarities (Gal 3); chaos (Gen 3–11) to peace (Rev 21–22).

11. Much more could be said here about appreciating human progress in the Bible. I'm grateful to Rob Bell for illuminating some of these examples of progress in the Bible. Consider a few passages: Exod 20:1–17 provided an ancient moral code. Numbers 35:6–15 demanded cities of refuge for those who accidentally killed someone to flee to and to dwell within so the Revenger (yes, this was an actual job title) could not exact revenge. Deuteronomy 21:10–14 established protocol allowing women who were captured in war to grieve for one month. Furthermore, if after taking a woman to bed the man found himself unhappy with the woman, he was prohibited from selling her and he was instructed to let her go wherever she wished. I know this is horrifying, but stick with me. Romans 14–15 differentiated between strong and weak consciences when it came to eating clean and unclean food, and it encouraged acceptance of the "other" who ate differently. In Philemon, Paul wrote to a slave owner named Philemon and asked him to receive back a runaway slave named Onesimus, not as a slave but as a brother. With these passages

CHAPTER 2. A GOOD BIBLE STORY

A fourth feature of the table this interpretation of the Bible story sets is a Divine pattern for transformation

The paradigmatic pattern of Jesus' life—in all four Gospels—is life, death, and resurrection.

    Life,

        Death,

            and Resurrection.

This Divine pattern demonstrates how we humans slowly grow up into all wisdom, knowledge, and ultimately, love. It looks like this:

We live.

We die.

We resurrect.

Isn't that exactly how it happens?

---

in mind, as terrible as they seem to us today, it should be observed that these were movements forward in the world. An ancient moral code in the midst of violent tribalism, was a movement forward. Refuge for the innocent when a Revenger was allowed to exact revenge, was a movement forward. Allowing space for a woman to grieve and to be set free as opposed to sold, was a movement forward. Making room for differences when it came to clean and unclean food, was a movement forward. Receiving back a runaway slave as a brother instead of as a slave, was a movement forward. Of course, these movements do not go far enough. How about just putting an end to the notion and role of a Revenger, or treating women as human beings instead of property, or making room for differences beyond clean and unclean food, or abolishing slavery altogether? Yes, of course! But you see, to do so would have been unconscionable. Such consciousness about human rights and dignity were beyond ancient Israel, the apostle Paul, and the early church. However, in their day and age, these movements were radical, good, and compassionate steps forward. It's these biblical movements forward that invite today's readers of the Bible to faithfully continue in its staid, encouraging ever-more forward progress, today.

PART I. A BIT ON GOOD

We see things a certain way. That way of seeing eventually dies. And a new way of seeing rises and becomes what we could rightly call "new life."

Or, we think a certain way. That way of thinking eventually dies. And a new way of thinking rises and becomes what we could rightly call "new life."

Or, we do things a certain way. That way of doing things eventually dies. And a new way of existing rises and becomes what we could rightly call "new life."

Is there any other way to grow, to transform, to evolve, to become?

I don't think there is.

> It is all life, death, and resurrection—
>> Again and again.
>> Moment by moment.
>> Season by season.
>> Year by year.
>> Developmental stage by developmental stage.

We—individually and as a species—grow up into all wisdom, goodness, and ultimately, love, through life, death, and resurrection.

It's this way of becoming that leads to the flourishing and wholeness of all things, which is what we see at the end of the story in Rev 22:

> Then the angel showed me the river of the water of life, bright as crystal, flowing from throne of God.

I'd like to pause, just for a moment.

CHAPTER 2. A GOOD BIBLE STORY

Sometimes I find it helpful to replace the word "God" with the word "Love." It's a connection we find in 1 John 4:7 where we read that "God is Love." And so, from Rev 22,

> Then the angel showed me the river of the water of life, bright as crystal, flowing from throne of Love and of the Lamb through the middle of the street of the city. On either side of the river is the tree of life with its twelve kinds of fruit, producing its fruit each month; and the leaves of the tree are for the healing of the nations. Nothing accursed will be found there any more. But the throne of Love and of the Lamb will be in it, and Love's servants will worship Love; they will see Love's face, and Love's name will be on their foreheads. And there will be no more night; they need no light of lamp or sun, for the Lord Love will be their light, and they will reign forever and ever.[12]

How good is that?

A sacred story encouraging patience—becoming takes time?

A sacred story instilling hope—we can grow?

A sacred story reflecting humankind's slow march forward—we are making progress?

A sacred story embodying an anti-Adam wisdom grasping pattern for transformation and growth—life, death, and resurrection?

A sacred story into which Jesus invites, "Come, follow after me"?

That's a truly great story. It's a story of hope. It's a story of possibility. It's a story of becoming, over time, the fullness of the knowledge of God, which is Love itself.

12. Rev 22:1–5.

Chapter 3. A Good Gospel Story

This chapter explores stories told about the gospel. For those of us who identify as Christian, there is perhaps no word more important than "gospel." Yet, depending on a person's understanding of the gospel story, the meaning of gospel significantly changes.

The Story We Have Been Told

Due to Adam and Eve's sin—which was eating from a tree called "The Knowledge of Good and Evil"—humans are inherently depraved, separated from God, and in need of salvation. Thankfully, Jesus, the son of God, came to earth and became a savior by dying on a cross and shedding his blood, which has the power to forgive sins. Anyone who places their trust in Jesus' shed blood for the forgiveness of their sins is saved. To be saved means a person will spend eternity in bliss, in a place called "heaven," rather than eternity in torment, in a place called "hell."

The Table This Story Sets

According to this gospel story, humans are depraved. To be depraved is to be morally corrupt and intrinsically wicked. Of course, this human state can be altered by trust in Jesus' shed blood for the forgiveness of sins, but let's just sit with this part of the story for a moment.

CHAPTER 3. A GOOD GOSPEL STORY

*A first feature of the table this gospel story sets
is guilt and shame.*

Imagine you're a child growing up in a church, hearing this story again and again. Without trust in Jesus,

> you are sinful,
>
> your heart is wicked,
>
> and your desires are ungodly.

Subtly, over time, this story sinks deeper and deeper into your bones, doesn't it?

So deep.

You aren't good. In fact, at the deepest part of yourself you are bad, evil, wicked. Do you see how this story sets a table of shame and guilt?

> I am sullied.
>
> I am racked with sin.
>
> The deepest parts of myself are corrupt.

*A second feature of the table this gospel story sets
is a distrust of self.*

If you live within this story for long enough, it begins to have an impact on your thoughts about that small, quiet voice inside of yourself. Some people call it your "knowing." We all know this knowing. But have the stories you have been told, taught you to trust it? Can you trust that knowing that feels afraid or brave or hesitant or excited? Can you trust that knowing that points you in a direction or tells you something about yourself? Over time, this gospel story causes great suspicion about our own, intuitive

PART I. A BIT ON GOOD

knowing. For some, that suspicion grows so grand they begin to distrust everything about themselves.

Taking this feature a step further, this gospel story externalizes knowing. For if we can't trust ourselves to be good, then we have to place our trust in people and systems outside of ourselves that hold all of the power in telling us what's good.

I remember such strong feelings of self-doubt about my own goodness in my younger years. At times, these intense feelings of negativity were baffling. I had been told that after trusting in Jesus I was redeemed and good, through and through. Ah! But the fall of Adam and Eve—and its associated guilt—sat so deep inside of me that not even Jesus could save me from distrusting myself.

I want to be fair and balanced. The table this gospel story sets isn't all bad. It absolutely rouses gratitude. Gratitude for

> the forgiveness of sins,
>
> the conversion from wickedness to righteousness,
>
> and the promise of eternal bliss in a place called "heaven."

So. Much. Gratitude.

However, lurking right beside the gratitude are other experiences, such as fear. Fear for

> family
>
> and friends
>
> and humanity
>
>> who do not trust
>>
>> in Jesus.

And this fear rouses worry:

CHAPTER 3. A GOOD GOSPEL STORY

What am I to do?

I must do something!

A third feature of the table this gospel story sets is relational manipulation and emotional violence.

Several months ago I was on vacation, sitting on a deck, looking out over an exquisite mountain range. After a few minutes I lost sight of the view as I overheard a person on the deck above me on some kind of group phone call or online meeting explaining how to save their friends and family members from hell. Having been raised with a similar story, I understood that this person truly believed their strategic conversation was loving. However, talking about shaping a conversation to get to the point they wanted to make? That's manipulation. Admonishing courage to tell their unsaved friends and family members they're headed to eternal torment in a place called "hell" if they don't trust in Jesus' shed blood? That's violence. It's a table of manipulation and violence as a result of a gospel story still told by many people today.

A common response I hear from those who believe in and tell this gospel story is that it may be difficult to hear, but it's biblical. At least two problems occur due to this way of thinking. First, the word "gospel" means "good news." A story explaining humans are depraved and in need of shed blood to satiate a Divinity who lets the few who believe into heaven while sending the majority of humans to hell forever, is not good news. Second—and far more surprising to people—is this particular gospel story isn't biblical, in a straightforward way.

The path to the gospel story we have been considering is a mishmash of numerous Bible stories and verses woven together, profoundly shaped by culture over the past few hundred years, and uniquely expressed in a Western, Protestant, Evangelical tradition that has reduced good news down to a statement to be believed or else.

PART I. A BIT ON GOOD

The Story We Need to Hear

This brings me to another gospel story that is much more ancient and biblically straightforward, which I believe has the potential to set a table that's truly good. To understand this gospel story, we need to go on a brief literary and historical journey.

Going back to the years around the life of Jesus, the first Roman Caesar, Julius, was said to have Divine origins. Because of this, he was sometimes called "the Divine Julius." When Julius's son, Augustus, came after Julius, it's of no surprise that he was considered to have some divinity in his blood. For this reason, it made sense to call Caesar Augustus "the Son of God."

If you grew up in the church, this may be astonishing. Jesus was not the first Son of God. This is very important to understanding the gospel story.

Caesars were also referred to as "saviors." "An inscription published in the year 9 BC for a calendar reform of the cities of Asia Minor, in the town of Priene, speaks the language of the imperial cult: there, the birth of Emperor Augustus, the 'Son of God,' is a 'birth of God,' bringing the 'Saviour' and creating 'peace.'"[1]

According to this ancient inscription, Caesar, the son of God, was a savior who brought about peace on earth.

Again, if you grew up in the church, this may be astonishing. Jesus was not the first savior who was said to bring about peace on earth. This is very important to understanding the gospel story.

---

1. Bibelhaus Erlebnis Museum, "Calendar Inscription." This Priene Calendar Inscription is a Greek inscription. It contains a decree issued by the council of Asia and now resides in the Berlin Museum. While on loan at Bibelhaus Erlebnis Museum, it's described as containing imperial cult language that precedes Christian motifs.

CHAPTER 3. A GOOD GOSPEL STORY

If all of this isn't interesting enough, here is where things get really interesting. The phrase "peace through victory" was a Roman phrase that described how the Caesars, the sons of God, saved the world. It took place like this:

> The greatest military to ever exist would go out and crush everyone who was not loyal to Rome. It would then kill, sometimes through crucifixion, anyone remaining who would not subjugate themselves to Roman rule.

Then:

> After new territory had been procured through massive violence, an announcement would be sent throughout the empire called "gospel," which can also be translated as "good news."[2] It was this good-news-gospel that declared the extension of peace in the world, by way of massive violence.

I realize this is a lot of obscure information. Here's a brief summary of Rome's good-news-gospel:

> Caesar,
> the son of God,
> is a savior,
> > who brings about peace on earth,
> > through violence.

As a capstone to this summary, it's important to know that a primary symbol for peace throughout Rome was a cross. With this information, Rome's good-news-gospel can be succinctly stated:

---

2. In the Greek, this word is εὐαγγέλιον, which is the same Greek word translated as either "gospel" or "good news" throughout the New Testament.

PART I. A BIT ON GOOD

> Caesar, the son of God, is a savior, who brings about peace on earth, through a cross.

Once again, if you grew up in the church, this may be astonishing:

> Jesus was not the first son of God.
>
> Jesus was not the first savior.
>
> Jesus was not the first who was said to bring about peace on earth through a cross.

That message was an already-existing, tried-and-true sentiment throughout the land into which Jesus was born. This is especially important to understanding the gospel story to which we now turn.

Beginning with the oldest of all the Gospels, the Gospel of Mark, we read these words in chapter 1, verse 1:

> The beginning of the good news of Jesus Christ, the Son of God.[3]

What do we have here? Well, let's begin by stating what we do not have. We do not have a brand new idea being birthed into the world. The good-news-gospel of Caesar Augustus, the son of God, who brings about peace on earth through violence symbolized by a cross, already existed.

This, you see, is the point. This is where the primary meaning of Jesus' good-news-gospel comes from, *if*—and this is important—*if* you make the correct interpretive turn. Unfortunately, many of us have been led to make the wrong turn. This wrong turn has resulted in Jesus' good-news-gospel becoming another Roman gospel, which sounds like this:

---

3. The Greek word used here is εὐαγγέλιον, which is translated as either "gospel" or "good news" throughout the New Testament.

CHAPTER 3. A GOOD GOSPEL STORY

Jesus, the Son of God, is a Savior who brings about peace on earth through a cross. Those who believe in this gospel will spend eternity in heaven; those who do not believe in this gospel will spend eternity in hell.

To use common medieval and modern-day Christian vernacular,

> Believe or else!

Tragically, this interpretive turn recasts the same old gospel of Rome in Jesus' name, and many have endured its violence.

An honest reading of the Gospel of Mark, as well as the other Gospels, clearly establishes Jesus as the anti-Caesar, not a mightier Caesar. From the very beginning, the good-news-gospel of Jesus was an intentional undoing; it was an intentional subversion of Rome's good-news-gospel.

With this historical context in mind, take a moment to imagine Caesar, the son of God, the savior, standing in his palace, unrolling a scroll, and declaring his most recent good-news-gospel shortly after conquering another kingdom:

> Good news, good news! Peace on earth through massive violence, which is symbolized throughout the land by a cross.

We're now set up to make the correct interpretive turn as Jesus declares his good-news-gospel, in Luke 4. Jesus walks into a synagogue, takes the scroll of Isaiah, unrolls it, and reads these words:

> The Spirit of the Lord is upon me,
> because [God] has anointed me
> to bring good news . . .[4]

---

4. Luke 4:18. The Greek word used here is again εὐαγγέλιον.

PART I. A BIT ON GOOD

And what is this good-news-gospel? Peace through massive violence? No. Ponder these subversive words:

> "The Spirit of the Lord is upon me,
> because [God] has anointed me
> to bring
> > good news to the poor.
>
> [God] has sent me to proclaim
> > release to the captives
> > and recovery of sight to the blind,
> > to let the oppressed go free,
> > to proclaim the year of the Lord's favor."
>
> And he rolled up the scroll, gave it back to the attendant, and sat down. The eyes of all in the synagogue were fixed on him. Then he began to say to them, "Today this scripture has been fulfilled in your hearing." All spoke well of him and were amazed at the gracious words that came from his mouth.[5]

The meaning of this moment is often lost on modern Christians, but it wasn't lost on Jesus' original audience. They knew exactly what he was doing. Jesus was casting himself as the anti-Caesar who would subvert the very soul of Rome's good-news-gospel with his own.

Before moving on, let's take a moment to notice what's missing from Jesus' good-news-gospel:

> Anything about humans being inherently depraved and separated from the Divine.
>
> Anything about the need for blood to receive the forgiveness of sins.

---

5. Luke 4:16–22.

CHAPTER 3. A GOOD GOSPEL STORY

Anything about heaven or hell as eternal destinations based on a person's belief.

As we can now appreciate, Mark's first words, "The beginning of the good news of Jesus Christ, the Son of God," and Jesus' declaration of that good news in Luke 4, were clearly intended as subversion. It's in this subversion that the goodness of Jesus' gospel lies.

The Table This Story Sets

Jesus' declaration of good-news-gospel insists on the creation of a table shaped by at least five features.

Jesus said, "The Spirit of the Lord is upon me, because [God] has anointed me to bring good news to the poor."[6]

> *One feature of the table this gospel story sets is truly good news for those who are poor.*

Jesus said, "[God] has sent me to proclaim release to the captives."[7]

> *A second feature of the table this gospel story sets is the release of those in captivity.*

Jesus said, "[God has sent me to bring] recovery of sight to the blind."[8]

> *A third feature of the table this gospel story sets is the healing of every ailment.[9]*

---

6. Luke 4:18a.
7. Luke 4:18b.
8. Luke 4:18c.
9. As understood today, blindness isn't necessarily an ailment. To insist it is, is subject to ableism. In this ancient text, the healing of blindness is a metaphor representing many different kinds of healing.

PART I. A BIT ON GOOD

Jesus said, "[God has sent me] to let the oppressed go free."[10]

A fourth feature of the table this gospel story sets is the alleviation of oppression.

And finally, Jesus said, I'm here "to proclaim the year of the Lord's favor."[11] The year of the Lord's favor refers to Jubilee as it's described in Lev 25. Put simply, Jubilee declared to every person, "The favor of the Lord upon you," and it held extraordinary benefits for everyone. Although Jubilee only occurred every fifty years in Jewish tradition, Jesus' good-news-gospel was the declaration of Jubilee favor and benefits, now.

A fifth feature of the table this gospel story sets is the unrestrained declaration of Divine favor upon every person.

I have found that this good-news-gospel story sets truly loving, inclusive, and passionately good tables. This good-news-gospel story also helps us to evaluate all other gospel stories. For example, any declaration of a gospel that adds to burdens, amplifies fear, increases alienation, or magnifies ifs, ands, or buts to curry favor is not revolutionary gospel. Gospels like these do not set loving tables and are, quite literally, anti-Christ. For Jesus, the Son of God, is a Savior who declares subversive news that's truly good for every person.

The subversiveness of this good-news-gospel hits its crescendo when Jesus, rather than wielding power and might, is crushed by power and might. In doing so, Jesus transforms Rome's violent cross into a symbol of Divine self-giving and solidarity with every person who is crushed by empire.

---

10. Luke 4:18d.
11. Luke 4:19.

CHAPTER 3. A GOOD GOSPEL STORY

How good is that?

If you grew up with the first gospel story I told, you may be wondering about the spiritual side of the gospel. This wondering is usually related to theological ideas on salvation, atonement, and the afterlife. The next chapter addresses salvation. Chapter 5 addresses atonement. Chapter 6 addresses the afterlife. However, before getting to those chapters, I want to briefly consider the word "spiritual." The word "spiritual" refers to the nonmaterial and nonphysical aspects of our human existence. A few aspects of the spiritual—beyond modern Christianity's emphasis on depravity and getting souls into heaven—include experiences such as

> awe and wonder,
>> mercy and grace,
>>> gratitude and peace.

It's consequential spiritual experiences like these that the first gospel story often minimizes and even harms. Fortunately, a more ancient and biblical gospel story exists. It's a gospel story that declares:

> Good news to the poor!
>
> Release to the captives!
>
> Recovery of sight for the blind!
>
> Let the oppressed go free!
>
> The year of the Lord's favor!

The proclamation and manifestation of this gospel story to every person, in every time—no matter ideology, race, sexual orientation, gender identity, education, occupation, financial bracket, or citizenship status—is truly good news. It's good news that imbues spirituality with

> awe and wonder,
>> mercy and grace,
>>> gratitude and peace.

A sixth feature of the table this gospel story sets is spiritual health and vitality.

Chapter 4. A Good Salvation Story

To begin this chapter, it's going to be helpful to split some theological hairs, which aren't often distinguished in our Christian storytelling.

For many, the words "gospel," "salvation," and "atonement" are understood to be synonyms. That's to say, these words are often used interchangeably. For example, many Christians today would say

> to believe in the gospel is to be saved,
> or, to be saved is to believe in the gospel,
> and, the gospel is the work of atonement,
> and so, atonement is the way in which a person is saved,
> and that's the gospel.

Clear as mud?

To try and be clear, these three words are associated. They just aren't the same thing. Gospel, salvation, and atonement are not synonyms. Let me give three brief—but technical—definitions:

> Gospel is the declaration of good news.
> Salvation is being saved from a predicament.
> Atonement is the reconciliation of estranged parties.

With these technical differences in mind, "salvation" is being saved from a predicament. For many people today, the predicament requiring salvation is twofold:

> Predicament #1: Because of original sin, a person is depraved and in need of forgiveness.
>
> Predicament #2: Because of original sin, a person is destined to eternal torment in hell.

The Story We Have Been Told

We're now ready to hear the salvation story as it's told by many Christians today. It goes like this:

> A person is saved by believing in Jesus' shed blood for the forgiveness of sins.
>
> A person who receives forgiveness of sins is saved from eternal torment in hell.

That's the story.

Because of original sin, a person is depraved and in need of forgiveness, which comes by believing in Jesus' shed blood on a cross. Belief in Jesus' shed blood results in the forgiveness of sins and the promise of eternal life in heaven.

Predicament:

> Sin and hell.

Salvation:

> Forgiveness and heaven.

That's the salvation story according to many people today.

CHAPTER 4. A GOOD SALVATION STORY

The Table This Story Sets

Notice the kind of table this salvation story sets in the lives of people.

> *One feature is a deeply embedded belief in the inherent wickedness of humans.*

I addressed a feature similar to this in chapter 2. It rises from the idea of original sin. Rather than repeat myself in explaining how original sin is a misinterpretation of the Bible story's inciting incident and of Rom 5:12, I'd like to delve further into how this way of seeing the world is horrifying.

To be depraved is to be morally corrupt and wicked through and through. This way of seeing people has an impact. For example, if every person is depraved through and through, then we cannot possibly expect goodness from the lives of those who are "unsaved." Quite the opposite, in fact. If every person is depraved through and through, then what we must expect from unsaved humans is corruption and wickedness again and again. Not only is this a horrifying way of existing in the world, but it's at odds with our lived experiences of those who are "unsaved":

> Is your experience of unsaved children corruption and wickedness through and through?
>
> Is your experience of unsaved neighbors corruption and wickedness through and through?
>
> Is your experience of unsaved coworkers, acquaintances, and strangers corruption and wickedness through and through?
>
> Is your experience of unsaved people groups corruption and wickedness through and through?

If we're being honest, the answer is clearly no.

PART I. A BIT ON GOOD

A second feature of the table this salvation story sets is unreasonable logic.

Since humans are not corrupt and wicked through and through—because original sin doesn't exist—a salvation story in which humans deserve to go to a place of eternal torment, forever, is irrational.

For a moment, I want to notice how strange the word "deserve" is here. In this particular salvation story, we are taught to think humans—created by God but corrupted by something Adam and Eve did—deserve to go to a place of eternal torment, forever. How in the world does any human deserve that? This logic is similar to—but not nearly as horrifying as—saying a person deserves a lifetime in solitary confinement for something egregious that some other person did a few thousand years ago.

It's not fair.
It's not just.
It makes no sense.
It is unequivocally unreasonable.

A third feature of the table this salvation story sets is puzzling forgiveness.

According to this particular story, a person must believe in Jesus' shed blood for God to forgive their sins. Let's think about that.

> Throughout the Hebrew Scriptures God forgives people again and again.

Of course, a person deep in this particular salvation story will respond by saying something like, "Yes, but that's because God had Israel make sacrifices, which resulted in forgiveness. And that's why people need to trust in Jesus' shed blood to receive

CHAPTER 4. A GOOD SALVATION STORY

forgiveness, today." However, if that's true, then we should ask ourselves some questions:

> Why does God forgive Israelites without the offering of sacrifices?[1]
>
> Why was God forgiving non-Israelite people and nations who weren't part of Israel's sacrificial system throughout the Hebrew Scriptures?[2]
>
> Why was Jesus forgiving people before he died on a cross?[3]

Besides these points, does it even make sense that God needs Jesus' blood to forgive humans? Again, if you're deep in this particular salvation story, then you're forced to say *yes*. However, that's a misunderstanding of atonement, which I address in chapter 5.

For now, let's not miss the puzzling and tragic nature of this understanding of forgiveness. Say, for example, a kid across the street intentionally throws a baseball through the front window of my house. I return home to find the window broken, and so I have it fixed. Over the next few days that kid starts to feel really bad and he, eventually, knocks on my door. With tears in his eyes, he says, "I am so, so very sorry." In that moment I can feel how bad he feels. I really want to forgive him. And so, what do I do? Well, it's obvious, isn't it? I tell him to wait. I go and kill my own child. I then return to the front door to let him know everything is okay, I forgive him.

But is everything truly okay? Because for me to forgive a kid, I have to become a murderer. Does that make any sense at all? No. Yet, this is the very salvation story many Christians tell today.

---

1. Exod 34:7, Num 14:13, 2 Chr 7:14, Ps 103:12, Isa 43:25.
2. Isa 55:7, Jon 3:10, Matt 6:12, Mark 1:4, 11:25.
3. Matt 9:2, Mark 2:5, Luke 5:20.

PART I. A BIT ON GOOD

A fourth feature of the table this salvation story sets is the absence of a connection to Jesus' good-news-gospel.

As I shared in the last chapter, Jesus' good-news-gospel is clearly explained:

> Freedom from bondage.
>
> Healing for the sick.
>
> Release for the oppressed.
>
> God's favor on everyone.

However, this particular salvation story has nothing to do with Jesus' good-news-gospel. Because—according to this particular salvation story—the predicament is sin and hell, and the salvation is forgiveness and heaven.

That's a problem.

It's a problem that the salvation story many people tell today has no connection to Jesus' gospel in Luke 4. It's also a problem that this particular salvation story has nothing to do with Jesus' life or ministry prior to his crucifixion.

The Story We Need to Hear

Here's to a more robust and coherent salvation story that's truly good. To begin, a brief word study.

Salvation and its associated words—save, saved, saves, saving, and savior—occur nearly 500 times in the Bible.

The word "salvation" occurs about 127 times.

The words "saved," "saves," and "saving" occur about 300 times.

CHAPTER 4. A GOOD SALVATION STORY

The word "savior" occurs about 40 times.

Here's why that information is important. Many Christians think of salvation as a New Testament, and uniquely Jesus, concept. However, the majority of the Bible's salvation words—roughly two-thirds—occur in the Hebrew Scriptures. Outside of Daniel—one of the latest written books in the Hebrew Scriptures—no mention of individual life beyond death exists.[4] Furthermore, the mentioning of individual life beyond death in Daniel is nothing like today's Christian ideas about the afterlife.

What about the New Testament? At times, the concept of salvation is applied to the predicament of sin and the afterlife. However, it's applied to many more predicaments that have nothing to do with sin and the afterlife. For these reasons, it's indisputable to state that biblical salvation is about much more than forgiveness and the afterlife.

The Hebrew word for salvation is *yeshua*, which simply translates "help."[5]

The Greek word for salvation is *soteria*, which translates "deliverance" and "preservation."[6]

Based on these definitions, biblical salvation speaks to being saved from predicaments. As we'll now see, these predicaments are multifaceted throughout the Scriptures.

In the Hebrew Scriptures, salvation has three primary meanings.[7]

---

4. I address Daniel's reference to the afterlife in chapter 6.
5. Help, deliverance, salvation (*HALOT*, s.v. "ישׁע").
6. Deliverance, preservation, salvation (BDAG, s.v. "σωτηρία").
7. I find Marcus Borg's categorizing of salvation in the Hebrew Scriptures into these three categories to be concise and accurate (*Heart of Christianity*, 177).

First, there's salvation as liberation from bondage in Egypt:

> Thus the LORD *saved* Israel that day from the Egyptians.[8]
>
> Yet I have been the LORD your God ever since the land of Egypt; you know no God but me, and besides me there is no *savior*.[9]
>
> They forgot God, their *Savior*, who had done great things in Egypt.[10]

In these verses—and many more like them—God is described as being a savior who works salvation by rescuing Israel from bondage in Egypt.

A second kind of salvation in the Hebrew Scriptures is return from exile. After liberation from bondage in Egypt, Israel became a nation that was eventually conquered by Assyria, and then by Babylon, and then by Persia. During captivity in Persia, God moved the heart of Persia's king—King Cyrus—and he allowed Israel to make a return to the land. About this salvation of return from Israel's exile in Persia, we read,

> When you pass through the waters, I will be with you; and through the rivers, they shall not overwhelm you; when you walk through fire you shall not be burned, and the flame shall not consume you. For I am the LORD your God, the Holy One of Israel, your *Savior*.[11]
>
> I bring near my deliverance, it is not far off, and my *salvation* will not tarry.[12]

---

8. Exod 14:30.
9. Hos 13:4.
10. Ps 106:21.
11. Isa 43:2–3.
12. Isa 46:13.

CHAPTER 4. A GOOD SALVATION STORY

In these verses, God is described as being a savior who works salvation by helping Israel return to the land.

A third kind of salvation in the Hebrew Scriptures is rescue from peril. This is the primary meaning of salvation in the psalms. Salvation appears in the psalms more than any other book in the Bible:

> O LORD my God, in you I take refuge; *save* me from all my pursuers, and deliver me, or like a lion they will tear me apart; they will drag me away, with no one to rescue.[13]

> But I am lowly and in pain; let your *salvation*, O God, protect me.[14]

> For [God] stands at the right hand of the needy, to *save* them from those who would condemn them to death.[15]

In these verses, the psalmist cries out for God's salvation, which includes deliverance from enemies, pain, and death.

Let's summarize:

> Salvation speaks to being saved from predicaments.
>
> The predicament out of which God works salvation is multifaceted.
>
> In the Hebrew Scriptures:
>> Salvation is liberation from bondage.
>>
>> Salvation is return from exile.
>>
>> Salvation is rescue from all kinds of peril.

---

13. Ps 7:1–2.
14. Ps 69:29.
15. Ps 109:31.

PART I. A BIT ON GOOD

Notice, nothing here about blood for the forgiveness of sins or ensuring life in heaven as opposed to hell.

Progressing to the Gospels, this multifaceted salvation from the Hebrew Scriptures wonderfully coheres with Jesus' declaration of a good-news-gospel.

Liberation from bondage?

In Luke 4, part of Jesus' gospel is the declaration of captives released and the oppressed set free. And throughout Jesus' ministry he releases captives and frees the oppressed.

Return from exile?

Jesus says again and again, "Repent, for the kingdom of heaven is at hand." The idea of the kingdom of heaven at hand would have been an encouragement to Jews living under the boot of the Roman Empire. According to Jesus throughout the Gospels, this kingdom belongs to the least, the last, the children, and the lowly.

Furthermore, according to Jesus, every person can access this loving kingdom through repentance. The word "repentance" has two primary meanings, and its primary meaning in Hebrew is "return."[16] It's a return we all need to make, every once in a while. Have you ever lost your way? Have you ever lost your very self? Have you ever taken stock of your life and thought, "Some time ago I stopped living in ways that matter the most"? Biblically speaking, that's a kind of exile. It's to this exile that Jesus admonishes, "Repent," which means, it's time to return home. And like God who promises to help guide Israel on their journey home in the book of Isaiah, we observe Jesus, in the Gospels, helping people to make that same journey into God's loving kingdom of heaven, at hand.

---

16. Repent, turn around, restore, refresh (*HALOT*, s.v. "שׁוּב").

CHAPTER 4. A GOOD SALVATION STORY

Rescue from peril?

In Luke 4, part of Jesus' gospel is the declaration of healing. And throughout Jesus' ministry he heals, again and again.

The Table This Story Sets

This multifaceted salvation story includes so much goodness.

> *One feature of the table this salvation story sets is biblical congruence.*

The various kinds of salvation we observe God working in the Hebrew Scriptures are the same kinds of salvation we see Jesus working throughout his life and ministry. This congruence tells us we're on the right track in our understanding of biblical salvation.

> *A second feature of the table this salvation story sets is truly good and desperately needed salvation.*

We live in a world where people are in political, economic, and religious bondage. How good and necessary is a salvation that's intentional about setting humans free?

I would say it's very good and very necessary, wouldn't you?

We live in a world where literal and existential exile exists. Millions of people are quite literally exiled from their homelands. And many people are existentially exiled—experiencing a lack of belonging, or sincere fragmentation, or incredible suspicion about God's pervasive and abiding love. How good and necessary is a salvation that's intentional to help, nurture, and work for people to return home?

I would say it's very good and very necessary, wouldn't you?

Finally, we live in a world where people are in all kinds of peril. How good and necessary is a salvation that's intentional about helping and healing?

I would say it's very good and very necessary, wouldn't you?

A third feature of the table this salvation story sets is spiritual health and vitality.

I concluded the last chapter by explaining this very point. I'd like to conclude this chapter by making a similar point in relation to a truly good salvation. Remember, the word "spiritual" refers to the nonmaterial and nonphysical aspects of our humanity. A few aspects of that which is spiritual, therefore, includes consequential human experiences such as awe and wonder, mercy and grace, gratitude and peace.

With this in mind, when a person is saved from any kind of bondage or exile or peril, some of that person's spiritual reality includes an increase of awe and wonder, mercy and grace, gratitude and peace. For certainly, when a person is saved from bondage, their spiritual life brims with elation. When a person is saved from exile, their spiritual life overflows with gratitude. And when a person is saved from peril, their spiritual life is transfixed by a deeper sense of peace.

An understanding of salvation that's congruent with the depth and breadth of the salvation we see throughout the Scriptures?

A salvation that's truly good and desperately needed in the world today?

A salvation that resolves very real predicaments, resulting in spiritual health and vitality here and now?

CHAPTER 4. A GOOD SALVATION STORY

Wouldn't that be a salvation worth entering into and enacting with our very lives?

It's this very salvation that the life of Jesus invites us to work out in the world, until love becomes so manifest that predicaments, out of which humans need salvation, no longer exist.

Part II. A Bit on Evolution

Evolution is a scientific theory that explains the process by which living organisms develop. In biology, this refers to heritable advancement such as mutation and genetic recombination, but the word also encapsulates the evolution of consciousness. "Throughout the ages life has constructed organisms of ever greater complexity, and with this increased complexity the organism has also shown an increase in consciousness."[1]

An increase.
In.
Consciousness.

That's exactly what we noticed in chapter 2, "A Good Bible Story." In the Bible, we bear witness to humankind's conscious increase—from law to love, obedience to grace, differences to similarities, and chaos to peace. It's this realization of conscious increase in the Bible that beckons us to continue on that path of trajectory, to participate in that which is truly good, today.

While part 1 focused on that which is good in the Bible, the gospel, and salvation, part 2 explores the evolution of Christian theology on atonement and the afterlife. As we'll see, an exploration of Christian theology throughout the Bible and church history

---

1. King, *Teilhard's Mysticism of Knowing*, 33.

reveals fluidity, not solidity. That's to say, throughout the Bible and church history, theologies on atonement and the afterlife evolve.

The notion that theology evolves may be unsettling, but it's honest. It's also necessary. For as humans increase in consciousness, the need to deconstruct theology articulated during earlier stages of consciousness is essential. Furthermore, as humans increase in consciousness, the need to reconstruct theology that coheres with the conscious perspectives of today is critical. Otherwise, we're forced to abide in a temple of archaic thought that makes less and less sense as everything continues to do that which it must do—evolve.

Although Darwin's theory of evolution is a product of the, quite recent, scientific revolution, the idea that humans have the capacity to increase in consciousness is deeply ancient. For example, consider Jesus' conversation with Nicodemus in John 3.

Nicodemus was a Pharisee, which meant he was an expert in Jewish law. More so, this meant he saw the world in a particular way and lived with intense commitment to that way. With this in mind, in the cover of dark, Nicodemus approaches Jesus and confesses to him that no one can do the signs and wonders he is able to do apart from the presence of God. In response, Jesus says, "Very truly, I tell you, no one can see the kingdom of God without being born from above."[2] This response leads to a conversation about the impossibility of a human returning to their mother's womb to be born again. Of course, Jesus isn't talking about biological birth. Rather, he's talking about conscious birth. About this particular kind of birth, Jesus says to Nicodemus,

> You should not be surprised at my saying, "You must be born again." The wind blows wherever it pleases. You hear its sound, but you cannot tell where it comes

2. John 3:3.

PART II. A BIT ON EVOLUTION

from or where it is going. So it is with everyone born of the Spirit.[3]

> Born of the Spirit
> Like wind
>> that blows
>> wherever it pleases
> And suddenly, everything
>> changes.

When was the last time you were born again? When was the last time the winds of your life changed and suddenly an idea or feeling or perspective birthed? Call it what you want—an aha, an epiphany, or being born again—you *evolved*. The wind blew and due to a whole bunch of intersecting circumstances—that you'd have a very difficult time explaining—your mind expanded, your heart opened, and your conscious increase forever changed the way you see it all.

Unsettling?
> Sure.

Exhilarating?
> Possibly.

Life changing?
> Absolutely.

Your conscious increase is your evolving self. It's as natural as biology and as miraculous as new life. The following two chapters explore similar evolution in theology on atonement and the afterlife, in the Bible and throughout church history.

---

3. John 3:7–8.

Chapter 5. An Evolutionary Atonement Story

The last chapter began by noticing that within today's Christianity, the words "gospel," "salvation," and "atonement" are often used interchangeably, and yet, technically speaking, they're different.

Let's review:

> Gospel is the declaration of good news.
>
> Salvation is being saved from a predicament.
>
> Atonement is the reconciliation of estranged parties.

This chapter explores the evolution in stories of atonement, which explain the reconciliation of estranged parties.

The Story We Have Been Told

According to many Christians today, the estranged parties include humans and God:

> Humans are separated from God due to original sin.

However, this estrangement can be remedied:

God will forgive the sins of those who trust in Jesus' shed blood on a cross.

Thus, the atonement story:

> A person who believes in Jesus' shed blood on a cross, for the forgiveness of their sins, is no longer separated from God but reconciled to God.

That's the atonement story.

The Table This Story Sets

Notice the kind of table this atonement story sets in the lives of people.

> *One feature is human separation from God.*

Human separation from God.

That's a profound statement, isn't it? It's a statement grounded in disgust. I am separated from the Divine because I am sinful, which is to say,

> Because I am sullied,
> Because I am defiled,
> Because I am blemished,
> > besmirched,
> > polluted,
> > damaged,
> > depraved,
> I am separated from God.

Let that way of seeing and being sink in for a while.

CHAPTER 5. AN EVOLUTIONARY ATONEMENT STORY

This is insidious ideology of the worst kind. Developmental theorists and psychologists agree, including Abraham Maslow who studied human motivation and need. Ultimately, Maslow famously explained a hierarchy of five essential human needs to flourish. One of those five hierarchies includes love and belonging.

Love and belonging.

What happens when a person exists in a reality in which love and belonging lack? Well, the findings are not good:[1]

Negative self-talk.

Ongoing comparison with others.

Difficulty setting boundaries.

Continuous striving.

Likelier to exist in abusive relationships.

In 1984, Father Thomas Keating invited a broad range of spiritual teachers from virtually all of the world's great wisdom traditions—Christian, Jewish, Buddhist, Hindu, Indigenous, and Islamic—to gather at St. Benedict's Monastery in Snowmass, Colorado. This came to be called the "Snowmass Conference." One key goal for the leaders' time at the Snowmass Conference was to investigate various points of agreement, for which they found eight.[2] One point of agreement that speaks directly against a feature of the table this atonement story sets reads,

> As long as the human condition is experienced as separate from Ultimate Reality, it is subject to ignorance and illusion, weakness and suffering.[3]

---

1. Allen et al., "Belonging," 2–7.
2. Miles-Yepez, *Common Heart*, xvii-xix.
3. Miles-Yepez, *Common Heart*, xvii.

PART II. A BIT ON EVOLUTION

Unfortunately, the atonement story many Christians tell today encourages this very ignorance and illusion, which results in much weakness and great suffering.

Of course, if you exist within this atonement story you're probably thinking, "Well sure, this may be difficult to believe, but it's in the Bible. It's just the way things are." However, as I have now shared a few times, this way of thinking is based on a misinterpretation of the Bible's inciting incident in Gen 3, and it's a misreading of Rom 5:12.

There is no such thing as original sin.

Furthermore, when we move out of the modern framework of biblical inerrancy, which I encouraged in chapter 1, a person no longer has to try and harmonize all of the Scriptures. Instead, by understanding the Bible to be an inspired text written by humans, we're freed to make accommodations for the spiritual and intellectual limitations of the Bible's human authors. It's through this interpretive lens that we can appreciate how ancient people perceived a three-tiered universe in which

> God is up there in the sky,
> humans are here on earth,
> and the devil is down there, in the earth.

For this reason, at one point in human existence, it was very easy to perceive of God being at a distance from humans. However, even this perspective is at odds with other perspectives within the Bible:

> God with the patriarchs.
> God with Moses.
> God with the prophets.
> God with humans, in Jesus.

CHAPTER 5. AN EVOLUTIONARY ATONEMENT STORY

> God with tax collectors and sinners, in Jesus.
>
> God with that rascal, Judas Iscariot, in Jesus.

And let us not forget about passages such as Acts 17:28, which reads,

> For in God we live and move and have our being.

Or from Eph 4:6, which reads,

> One God and Father of all, who is above all and through all and in all.

And so, which is it? Is God with us or is God separate from us? We should at least wonder, shouldn't we?

> Perhaps God is always and pervasively with us.
>
> Perhaps it's we humans who think God is separate.

If this is closer to the nature of Ultimate Reality, then atonement isn't actually something God needs. Instead, atonement is something we humans need. I'll return to this idea in just a bit.

> *A second feature of the table this atonement story sets is God's frightening and strange need for blood to forgive sins.*

Within Christianity, the idea that God needs blood to forgive sins comes out of the institution of Israel's sacrificial system in the last half of Exodus and the book of Leviticus. But again—through the lens of accommodation—was this God's need or Israel's thoughts about what God needs? I believe it's clear: this is all about what ancient Israel thought God needed. In fact, this is similar to what many ancient people thought. Many ancient people believed they needed to make sacrifices—blood sacrifices in particular—to satiate the divinities.

Fortunately, most people no longer think like this. Even within Judaism, bloody sacrifices are no longer being offered to God at the Temple Mount. Yet, many Christians today continue to think God needs blood to forgive sins. They'll point to the second half of Exodus and the book of Leviticus for their proof. Furthermore, they'll point to the writings of Paul, who often explains God's need for blood sacrifice to forgive sins.

All of this leads us to a very important question that seems obvious but isn't often talked about, which is *why*? Why does Paul excessively explain God's need for blood sacrifices to forgive sins? Well, if you read the Bible through the framework of inerrancy, the answer is "Because God said so!" But if you're freed to read the Bible through the lens of accommodation, the answer is "Because Paul was a Pharisee."

The realization that Paul was a Pharisee changes everything because Pharisees were experts in the law who had a special interest in Israel's purity rituals. Think about this with me:

> The Pharisee Paul has his vision of Jesus.
>
> The Pharisee Paul becomes a follower of Jesus.
>
> The Pharisee Paul needs to make sense of Jesus' death on a cross, in light of how he sees the world, which is through Israel's purity rituals.

This, you could say, was a very real predicament out of which Paul needed salvation. It's for this reason that throughout Paul's writings we bear witness to him trying to make sense of Jesus' death on the cross through his way of seeing the world—through Israel's purity rituals.

CHAPTER 5. AN EVOLUTIONARY ATONEMENT STORY

For the converted Pharisee Paul, this is the primary—not only—meaning of atonement. For the converted Pharisee Paul, the shedding of Jesus' blood on the cross for the forgiveness of sins was a necessary form of salvation due to his pharisaical predicament, which required sacrifices to please God.[4] It's this connection between Paul's pharisaical need for sacrifices to please God and the crucifixion of Jesus that results in Paul's experience of reconciliation—atonement—with God.

Is this the primary meaning of atonement? Well, if you see the world through the lens of Israel's ancient purity rituals—like the Pharisee Paul—then, yes. This is a very helpful way to make sense of Jesus' crucifixion. However, for the majority of us who don't exist within Paul's world view, this kind of meaning-making is both strange and frightening.

As I shared in the last chapter, it's strange because God was forgiving people before the sacrifices were established in the second half of Exodus. It's strange because God was forgiving non-Israelite people and nations who weren't even part of Israel's sacrificial system. And it's strange because Jesus himself was forgiving people before he died on a cross. For reasons like these, Christians today should be capable of imagining an economy of forgiveness, through which God extends mercy again and again, without the need for bloody sacrifice.

Besides God's need for blood being strange, it's also frightening. The thought that God needs blood to forgive sins is an ancient and barbaric way of understanding the Divine.

I'd like to retell an illustration I told in the last chapter, with a little more elaboration.

---

4. This particular aspect of atonement is best called "propitiation," which comes from the Greek root ἵλεως: being favorably disposed, with implication of overcoming obstacles unfavorable to a relationship (BDAG, s.v. "ἵλεως"). According to Paul, propitiation comes by Jesus' shed blood.

PART II. A BIT ON EVOLUTION

Let's say a kid across the street intentionally throws a baseball through the front window of my house. I return home to find the window broken, and so I have it fixed. Over the next few days that kid starts to feel really bad and he, eventually, knocks on my door. With tears in his eyes, he says, "I am so, so very sorry." In that moment I can feel how bad he feels. I really want to forgive him. And so, what do I do? It's obvious, isn't it? I tell him to wait. I go and kill my own child. I then return to the front door to let him know everything is okay, I forgive him.

But is everything truly okay? Because for me to forgive a kid, I have to become a murderer. Does that make any sense at all? No. Yet, this is the very atonement story many Christians tell today.

Taking this illustration a little further, in this story I am the one who represents God and the child is the one who represents humans asking God for forgiveness. About this, I'd like to ask a question. Is the child—who represents humans—to honestly believe I'm good, loving, and worth worshiping if I need the blood of my own child to forgive? I certainly hope not. Outside of a mindset that belongs to an ancient human, or to that of a Pharisee who sees life through purity rituals, this kind of thinking is utterly horrifying.

> *A third feature of the table this atonement story sets*
> *is a lack of appreciation for evolution*
> *in human consciousness.*

To think God is separate from humans is an ancient, three-tiered way of seeing the world.

To think God is separate from humans is a failure to acknowledge other passages—in the Bible—that explain God as above all, and through all, and in all.[5]

---

5. Acts 17:28, Eph 4:4–6, Col 1:15–17.

CHAPTER 5. AN EVOLUTIONARY ATONEMENT STORY

To think God needs blood to forgive sins is an ancient, uniquely pharisaical-Paul way of seeing the world.

And to think God needs the blood of a crucified and tortured Jesus to forgive the sins of humans makes no sense to a modern, civilized people.

To this last point, I imagine some Christians responding, "Sure, but more important than being a modern, civilized people is being a Christian people." Or, "Sure, but more important than being a modern, civilized people is being a people of the Bible."

Unfortunately, this response comes from a very particular atonement story that misses the fullness of atonement in the Bible and throughout church history.

The Story We Need to Hear

Let's begin with some important church history and biblical studies.

Church History Overview

Church history reveals an interesting evolution in the direction of atonement.[6]

> Over the centuries, some Christians thought atonement is primarily for God.
>
> However, other Christians thought atonement is primarily for humans.

---

6. This section is informed by Gustaf Aulén's *Christus Victor*; Helen Rhee's *Early Christian Literature*; Anselm of Canterbury's *Major Works*; Peter Abelard's *Ethical Writings*; and James Beilby and Paul R. Eddy's *Nature of the Atonement*.

PART II. A BIT ON EVOLUTION

However, other Christians thought atonement is primarily for the devil.

Seriously.

An early understanding of atonement in church history is that it was for the devil. This perspective is called "Christus Victor." According to this theory, Christ—Christus Victor—fights against and triumphs over the evil powers of this world, under which humankind is in bondage and suffering.[7] About this, third-century church father Irenaeus writes,

> For [Jesus] fought and conquered; for he was man contending for the fathers, and through obedience doing away with disobedience completely: for he bound the strong man [satan] and set free the weak.[8]

And from fifth-century monk and theologian Tyrannius Rufinus,

> For the object of that mystery of the incarnation which we expound just now was that the divine virtue of the Son of God, as though it were a hook concealed beneath the form and fashion of human flesh ... might lure on the Prince of this world [satan] to a conflict, to whom offering his flesh as bait, his divinity underneath might catch him and hold him fast with its hook, through the shedding of his immaculate blood.[9]

As wild as this perspective may seem to modern Christians, it's important to recognize there was a time—early in church history—during which people like Irenaeus and Rufinus, and the majority of their contemporaries, sincerely believed humankind was in literal bondage to satan, which kept them from relationship with the

---

7. Aulén, *Christus Victor*, 4.
8. Irenaeus, *Against Heresies* 3.18.6 (*ANF* 1:448).
9. Rufinus, *Commentary on the Apostles' Creed* 16 (*NPNF* 3:550).

Divine. For this reason, they emphasized an atonement story that explained an actual fight during which Jesus' death became "bait" that "caught satan and held him fast with its hook," thereby freeing humans to enter into relationship with God.

If you think this atonement story is strange, you're not alone. By the eleventh century, human consciousness evolved to a point that made this way of thinking difficult to appreciate. For example, consider Anselm of Canterbury's words:

> Supposing that the devil, or man, were his own master, or belonged to someone other than God, or was permanently in the power of someone other than God, then perhaps one could justly speak in those terms. However ... neither the devil nor man belongs to anyone but God.[10]

According to Anselm, no person or thing belongs to anyone other than God. He, therefore, rejects a satan-ward atonement, and he proposes a God-ward atonement, out of which the theory of satisfaction rises.

According to the theory of satisfaction, atonement is directed toward God because of original sin. Remember: humans are depraved and in debt, cannot repay their debt, and need to satisfy God, which occurs through belief in Jesus' shed blood on a cross.

Not only did this theory of satisfaction find support in the writings of the converted Pharisee Paul, but it was a unique solution to human consciousness throughout the ninth to fifteenth centuries, during which the system of feudalism flourished.[11] As a result, atonement as satisfaction became the prominent perspective on

---

10. Anselm of Canterbury, *Why God Became Man* 1.7 (Davies and Davies, 272).

11. Feudalism was a structure in which land was offered in exchange for various kinds of labor. These transactional offerings speak to a consciousness embedded in exchange, which perfectly situated humans throughout the ninth to fifteenth centuries to appreciate a theory of satisfaction.

atonement during the reformation, and it's been emphasized as the meaning of atonement, to this very day.

This is where things begin to get really interesting.

Around the same time as Anselm's theory of satisfaction lived Peter Abelard who, like Anselm, couldn't believe in a satan-ward atonement. However, having the mind of a theologian but the soul of a poet, Abelard couldn't bring himself to believe in Anselm's God-ward atonement either. Abelard thought satisfaction atonement was also absurd, and so he proposed a human-ward atonement called "humanistic theory."[12]

Stick with me here. This will come together soon.

According to humanistic theory, Jesus' death on the cross demonstrates the amazing depths of God's love for humanity. Although this theory didn't catch on at the time—outside of some Christian mystics—this perspective is slowly becoming a central focus on atonement today as Anselm's theory of satisfaction begins to crack and crumble in the lives of humans, in the twenty-first century.

With this context in mind, you may now be wondering, "Which one is it? Is atonement for the devil, for God, or for humans?" The answer that church history gives is this: atonement has been for all three—the devil, God, and humans. More so, atonement's focus—whether it be for the devil, God, or humans—has been based on the unique needs of humans existing within various stages of human consciousness.

Here's what I mean:

> In the first millennium CE, a majority of humans really believed they needed rescue from the devil. Their atonement story, therefore, emphasized Jesus' broken body as

12. Abelard, *Ethical Writings*, 38.

CHAPTER 5. AN EVOLUTIONARY ATONEMENT STORY

bait that hooked the devil and freed humans to enter into relationship with God.

In the second millennium CE, a majority of humans really believed they needed rescue from the debt of sin. Their atonement story, therefore, emphasized Jesus' shed blood on a cross to free humans from the debt of sin, allowing them to enter into relationship with God.

As we enter into the third millennium CE, more and more humans are finding these first two atonement stories to be absurd. Because of this, a growing need exists for an atonement story in which Jesus' crucifixion proves Divine Love. In other words, humans living today—in the twenty-first century—are in desperate need of a God who is with them and for them, proven by Divine Love poured out.

Biblical Studies Overview

If you abide within the first atonement story I shared, you may want to reply to this brief historical overview by saying, "So what? That's history. What does the Bible say?" The answer is that the Bible supports all three atonement stories.

The Bible supports an atonement for the devil:

> Since, therefore, the children share flesh and blood, [Jesus] likewise shared the same things, so that through death he might destroy the one who has the power of death, that is, the devil, and free those who all their lives were held in slavery by the fear of death.[13]

The Bible also supports an atonement for God:

---

13. Heb 2:14–15. See also 2 Tim 2:26, Rev 12:9–11, etc.

> ... justified as a gift by his grace through the redemption which is in Christ Jesus, whom God displayed publicly as a propitiation in his blood through faith.[14]

The Bible also supports an atonement for humans:

> But God proves his love for us in that while we still were sinners Christ died for us.[15]

Conclusions

A brief summary of this atonement story explains several things:

> First, atonement is the reconciliation of estranged parties.
>
> Second, Jesus' death on a cross is the focal point for the Christian work of reconciliation.
>
> Third, church history reveals an evolution in the direction of atonement depending on human consciousness—sometimes devil-ward, sometimes God-ward, and sometimes human-ward.
>
> Fourth, the Bible supports all three historical emphases on atonement.

Therefore, an honest, historical, and biblical atonement story explains,

> Jesus' death on the cross is the primary means through which human experiences of estrangement are reconciled in Christian life.

---

14. Rom 3:24–25a. See also Eph 1:7, Col 1:20, etc.
15. Rom 5:8. See also Rom 8:31–39, Gal 2:20, etc.

CHAPTER 5. AN EVOLUTIONARY ATONEMENT STORY

The Table This Story Sets

An appreciation for the evolution of Christian thought on atonement results in a table full of goodness.

> *One feature of the table this atonement story sets is ongoing relevance.*

In the first millennium CE, humans truly needed an atonement that helped to free them from a consciousness in which their very lives were in bondage to satan. For this reason, the story of Jesus' death on a cross was used to powerfully free humans from satan's grip so they could experience reconciliation to God.

In the second millennium CE, humans truly needed an atonement that helped to free them from a consciousness in which their very lives were in the debt of sin. For this reason, the story of Jesus' death on a cross was used to powerfully free humans from the burden of sin so they could experience reconciliation to God.

As we continue forward into this third millennium CE, many humans need an atonement to help free them from a consciousness in which they are depraved and separated from God. About this, let's not miss the irony. For many, today's need is the result of Christian storytelling on atonement from the previous millennia. The idea of original sin and its consequences are baked into the psyche of Christian culture, causing much confusion and tremendous fragmentation. Today, many people desperately need healing from this harm. An atonement story that emphasizes God's extravagant love could be the very balm this new millennium of Christianity needs.

> *A second feature of the table this atonement story sets is agency.*

Reflecting on some of the church history I shared, Anselm couldn't comprehend the idea of needing to be freed from the devil because he didn't think he was in bondage to the devil. What Anselm needed was forgiveness for the debt of sin, and so he emphasized that which he needed and it helped to reconcile him to God.

Similarly, Abelard—Anselm's contemporary—couldn't comprehend the idea of needing to be freed from the devil. However, he couldn't comprehend the idea of needing to be freed from the debt of sin through blood, either. What Abelard needed was proof of Divine Love, and so he emphasized that which he needed and it helped to reconcile him to God.

I'm not sure what stories you have been told throughout your life, and so I'm not sure how those stories have shaped your consciousness regarding estrangement from God. My sincere hope is that Jesus' death on a cross can be used to help nurture your sense of reconciliation to God, in ways you need.

A prescient example of this relevant atonement work is found in the life and writings of the extraordinary theologian James Cone. In his book *The Cross and the Lynching Tree*, he writes,

> I accept Delores William's rejection of theories of atonement as found in the Western theological tradition and in the uncritical proclamation of the cross in many black churches. I find nothing redemptive about suffering in itself. The gospel of Jesus is not a rational concept to be explained in a theory of salvation, but a story of God's presence in Jesus' solidarity with the oppressed, which led to his death on the cross.[16]

For Cone—a Black man who lived his life in the United States throughout the twentieth century—an atonement story in which God kills his own son on a tree was not good news. It was, in fact, horrifying news. He therefore rejected Anselm's atonement and the primary focus of atonement in Christianity throughout the second

---

16. Cone, *Cross and the Lynching Tree*, 150.

CHAPTER 5. AN EVOLUTIONARY ATONEMENT STORY

millennium by choosing to emphasize Divine solidarity with those who suffer, especially those who suffer by being lynched on trees. It's this Divine solidarity that brought Cone and many other Black Christians throughout the twentieth century a deep and abiding sense of God's presence with them as they endured racism and murder—sometimes, murder by lynching on trees.

A third feature of the table this atonement story sets is new frontiers.

The evolution of atonement's focus—in the Bible and throughout church history—invites us to consider new ways in which Jesus' death on a cross can be used to reconcile estranged parties yet to be emphasized or considered in Christian thought. For me, one area that stands out as desperately needed today is the reconciliation we read about in Eph 2:15–16, which reads,

> He [Jesus] has abolished the law with its commandments and ordinances, that he might create in himself one new humanity in place of the two, thus making peace, and might reconcile both groups to God in one body through the cross, thus putting to death that hostility through it.

Paul has in mind Jews and Gentiles, here. However, we can rightly extend this idea of two races to include any two kinds of people or groups of people who are divided:

Black and white people,

or queer and straight people,

or poor and rich people,

or undocumented and documented people,

or non-Christian and Christian people,

or *you fill in the blank* people.

PART II. A BIT ON EVOLUTION

Tragically, many of these divisions—and the resulting violence and harm these divisions cause—are due to Christian storytelling. Standing against this storytelling is a historical and biblical atonement story, unabashed in its audacious purpose: the reconciliation of all things.

> For in him [Jesus] all the fullness of God was pleased to dwell, and through him God was pleased to reconcile to himself all things, whether on earth or in heaven, by making peace through the blood of his cross.[17]

If your atonement story increases estrangement or intensifies alienation, please, let that story die. And in its place, let rise a relevant, profoundly necessary, and unequivocally good atonement story capable of carving out new frontiers in which the death of Jesus encourages and makes manifest desperately needed reconciliation, today.

---

17. Col 1:19–20.

Chapter 6. An Evolutionary Afterlife Story

According to many Christians today, what happens after a person dies is clear, concise, and incontrovertibly true. More so, these convictions about the afterlife are understood to be at the very center of why being a Christian is essential.

The Story We Have Been Told

The story goes like this: Those who believe in Jesus' shed blood for the forgiveness of their sins are destined to live out a conscious, embodied eternity in bliss in a place called "heaven." Those who do not believe in Jesus' shed blood for the forgiveness of their sins are destined to live out a conscious, embodied eternity in torment in a place called "hell."

That's the story.

Believe in Jesus' shed blood for the forgiveness of sins and you will live eternally in conscious, embodied bliss. Fail to believe in Jesus' shed blood for the forgiveness of sins and you will live eternally in conscious, embodied torment.

PART II. A BIT ON EVOLUTION

The Table This Story Sets

Notice the kind of table this afterlife story sets in the lives of people.

One feature is an empire story.

Remembering back to chapter 3, "A Good Gospel Story," any declaration of "good news" ending in "or else" is not the good-news-gospel of Jesus. As we observed in that chapter, any declaration adding to burdens, amplifying fear, increasing alienation, or magnifying ifs, ands, or buts to belong,

> is not revolutionary gospel,
>
> does not set loving tables,
>
> and is—according to Jesus' intentional Roman gospel subversion—anti-Christ.

For Jesus, the Son of God, is a Savior who declares subversive news truly good for every person. The fact that the very gospel of Rome that Jesus intentionally subverted has evolved into today's Christian gospel—believe, or else; always, or else—is one of the most scandalous and outrageous aspects of today's Christianity.

A second feature of the table this afterlife story sets is a horrifying and unjust story.

I'll begin with horrifying.

To believe in this afterlife story is to believe the majority of humans throughout human history will go to a place of conscious, embodied torment, forever.

Christians must think about this.

CHAPTER 6. AN EVOLUTIONARY AFTERLIFE STORY

To believe in a story in which the majority of humans throughout human history go to a place of conscious, embodied torment, forever, is truly horrifying.

It's also unjust.

It's unjust because it's inequitable. By this I mean some people will never get to hear this particular story, and so they won't even have a chance to believe in it. Furthermore, there will be many countless others who do hear about this story, but it won't make sense to them or for one reason or another they won't believe it.

It's also unjust because the notion of eternally conscious, embodied torment is inherently unjust. To alleviate this injustice, when Christians think about people going to hell, it helps to think about a really terrible person. Let's tease this out.

Take the worst person you can possibly think of throughout human history and imagine them in conscious, embodied torment. With this person in mind, I'd like to ask a question: At what point does this person's just torment become unjust? For example, let's imagine this person killed one hundred million people. And let's say for doing that they deserve conscious, embodied torment for a billion years per person. What happens after that person reaches this "just" punishment? Because, at some point in eternity, even this just punishment becomes unjust.

Here's another injustice. According to this afterlife story, the worst person in human history who "deserves" conscious, embodied torment for eternity is able to believe in Jesus' shed blood for the forgiveness of their sins, thereby ending up in bliss forever. All the while that really nice, generous, loving neighbor or coworker or friend or family member who fails to believe just the right thing will end up in conscious, embodied torment for much longer than one billion times one hundred million years.

PART II. A BIT ON EVOLUTION

It's because of unequivocal injustices like these that the early church and Catholic Church have wondered about the possibility of postmortem annihilation or purgatory or salvation, and yet, for the majority of Protestant Christians, such considerations are anathema. More so, they double down saying, "God said it, I believe it." Or, "It's in the Bible, I can't change it." All the while failing to realize their particular afterlife story doesn't actually reflect what we see in the Bible or in the early church, which I'll explain in just a moment.

A third feature of the table this afterlife story sets is worry and relational harm.

In the introduction to this book, I told a story about my sweet Sunday school teacher using the flannelgraph to warn us about hell. She placed flames at the bottom, laid a couple of the pretend kids over the flames, and went on to tell us about how we'd go into the flames forever if we didn't ask Jesus into our hearts.

This story deeply impacted my life. It became a lens through which I thought about God. It shaped my convictions about what was important. It caused me to worry a lot about friends and family members who didn't go to church. And I had many scary and sleepless nights as a result of that story.

I tell you this again because it reveals the natural way in which a person who believes in this afterlife story is forced live. For if a person truly believes in this horrifying story, then they must do absolutely anything necessary to get people—at least those they love—to believe.

Back in my early twenties, I was so engrossed in this afterlife story that it roused deep concern for my partner's grandparents. Although they were beautiful humans—full of gentleness and kindness—they weren't Christians. One evening, I went over to their house and I sat with them in their living room. However, rather

CHAPTER 6. AN EVOLUTIONARY AFTERLIFE STORY

than doing what is most human—connecting, talking, and allowing our life together to give shape to a shared experience—I forced upon them my afterlife story.

I could tell my story shocked them.

I could tell my story disturbed them.

True to their kind and gentle nature, they weren't interested in arguing. But they weren't interesting in believing, either. Instead, with their usual warmth and kindness, they thanked me for my time and walked me to the door.

I remember leaving their house. In my head, I told myself I did something brave, something good. But in my bones, my gut, I felt awful. If anyone should be telling stories for the purpose of instruction, it should have been them. Over eighty years of life. Nearly fifty years of marriage. The work of raising kids and surviving the Great Depression. They were the teachers of life and wisdom and love. Yet, there I was explaining to them their need to believe in shed blood to forgive their sins so they could go to heaven rather than conscious, embodied torment, forever.

It's one of the great regrets of my life.

Unfortunately, I didn't come to realize before they passed that my afterlife story didn't actually go back to the early church, to the life of Jesus, or to the Bible, and so I wasn't able to sit before them to say that I'm terribly sorry for the night I forced upon them a religious myth.

A fourth feature of the table this afterlife story sets is the false belief that today's afterlife story goes all the way back to Jesus.

PART II. A BIT ON EVOLUTION

Truly, that's what many Christians think. They sincerely believe their thoughts on the afterlife follow a direct line back to the early church, to the life of Jesus, and to the Bible itself.

But that's just not true.

It's a misconception.

What if I were to tell you this is what happens after death:

> The souls of Christian martyrs—people who are killed for their faith in Jesus—go directly to paradise.
>
> All others—saved and unsaved—go down to Hades, a literal place inside the bowels of the earth.
>
> Down in Hades are two enormous rooms.
>
>> One room is filled with the saved, who receive temporary rewards.
>>
>> The other room is filled with the unsaved, who receive temporary punishment.
>
> This is how things will continue until the great resurrection, at which point the saved will be reunited with flesh for eternal rewards and the unsaved will be reunited with flesh for eternal punishment.
>
> The End.

Thoughts about this afterlife story?

Besides being strange, no Christian today thinks Christian souls descend, in death, to Hades. However, the story I just told is exactly what the third-century church thought about the afterlife.[1] Everything I just explained was penned by the great Tertullian of Carthage—the third-century church father—who was

---
1. Tertullian, *Treatise on the Soul* 54–58 (ANF 3:230–35).

CHAPTER 6. AN EVOLUTIONARY AFTERLIFE STORY

instrumental in laying the groundwork for the church's articulation of its doctrine on the Trinity.[2]

These differences of thought on the afterlife are just a place to begin. If you read church thought on the afterlife post-Tertullian, you'll find an ongoing evolution of thought that eventually leads to that which many people think today. If you read church thought on the afterlife pre-Tertullian, you'll find an ongoing evolution of thought leading up to Tertullian's thoughts. And if you go back further—into the Bible—you'll find an evolution of thought on the afterlife that begins in the Hebrew Scriptures and continues on throughout the New Testament. This is because thought on the afterlife has an undeniable tradition of change and ongoing evolution, which I'll now explain with intentional brevity.

The Story We Need to Hear

To demonstrate the evolution of thought on the afterlife, this section will begin in the Hebrew Scriptures, proceed to Matthew and Mark, then to Luke and John, then to Paul's writings, then to Revelation, and it will conclude with church history.

Hebrew Scripture Thoughts on the Afterlife

Other than brief words in Daniel, which is among the last and latest books to be written, no mention of a personal afterlife exists in the Hebrew Scriptures.[3]

2. Tertullian, *Against Praxeas*.

3. Passages like Isa 26 and Ezek 37 refer to resurrection, but these explain a national resurrection of Israel, not individual resurrection. Furthermore, it's unclear in these passages whether the national resurrection is a resurrection of Israelites who have died or whether it's a rising of Israel as a nation. First Samuel 28 tells a story about Saul visiting the witch of Endor who summons the dead Samuel. In this story, the witch sees an appearance, Saul bows, and Samuel asks, "Why have you disturbed me by bringing me up?" (verse 15). This stand-alone text is strange and raises many more questions about the afterlife than it answers. This is because the story isn't about the afterlife but

87

PART II. A BIT ON EVOLUTION

Furthermore, in Daniel, the afterlife we read about is nothing like today's Christian thoughts on the afterlife:

> But at that time your people shall be delivered, everyone who is found written in the book. Many of those who sleep in the dust of the earth shall awake, some to everlasting life, and some to shame and everlasting contempt. Those who are wise shall shine like the brightness of the sky, and those who lead many to righteousness, like the stars forever and ever.[4]

According to this passage,

> many people who sleep in the dust will awake,
>
> some will awake to everlasting life and some to shame and everlasting contempt,
>
> and those who are wise shall shine like the brightness of the sky.

That's it. That's the exhaustive explanation on the afterlife in the Hebrew Scriptures.

> Nothing here about every person rising—just some waking.
>
> Nothing here about rewards or punishments—just undefined contempt or life, for some.

---

about Saul's continued attempts to manipulate circumstances to accommodate his desires. In 2 Kgs 2, Elijah ascends to heaven in a chariot of fire. Similar to the story in 1 Samuel, the narrative point isn't about an afterlife. Instead, it's about the end of Elijah's prophetic work and the beginning of Elisha's. Furthermore, throughout Jewish tradition, the focus of Elijah's ascension is on Elijah's return ushering in the reign of messiah on earth rather than ascension to heaven. Lastly, whatever one makes of these unusual stories in 1 Samuel and 2 Kings, what is clear is that they are unlike contemporary Christian thought on the afterlife. If anything, they contradict contemporary Christian thought on the afterlife because they precede the death and resurrection of Jesus. Filled with the "fallen nature" of original sin, they should be unable to enter heaven.

4. Dan 12:1b–3.

CHAPTER 6. AN EVOLUTIONARY AFTERLIFE STORY

> Nothing here about places called "heaven" or "hell"—just some shining like the brightness of the sky and like the stars forever.
>
> And certainly, nothing here about blood or the forgiveness of sins to live in eternal bliss as opposed to eternal torment.

This passage rouses two important questions.

First question: Why are Daniel's thoughts on the afterlife so vague and undefined in comparison to the church's thoughts today?

First answer: Daniel is just the beginning of an ever-increasing evolution of thought on the afterlife in the Bible.

Second question: Why is there nothing on the afterlife until we get to one of the latest written books in the Hebrew Scriptures?

Second answer: It isn't until Israel is living under the boot of the Babylonian Empire that Israel begins asking questions:

> Is this where we're going to live out our lives?
>
> Is this how our children and loved ones will experience the entirety of their lives?
>
> Is this where we will suffer and eventually die, under the boot of the Babylonian Empire?
>
> What about justice?

It's through questions like these that we bear witness to Israel's evolving consciousness, which began pondering a novel idea: the possibility of justice after death.

It can certainly be argued that justice is a value in the Hebrew Scriptures much earlier than Daniel. However, this value for justice doesn't take on the ideological form of an afterlife—as a way to make up for a lack of justice—until Daniel.

This awareness is significant. It's here in Daniel that we bear witness to the beginning of a new kind of biblical salvation. Remember, salvation refers to being saved from a predicament. And the predicament in Daniel is the lack of justice in this life. To which Daniel responds, there will be justice for some who die.

Contextualizing Thoughts on the Afterlife in the New Testament

According to the ancient Jewish historian Josephus, three primary perspectives on the afterlife existed during the life of Jesus.[5] One perspective belonged to the Essenes. The Essenes held to a Greek view of the afterlife, believing the body was impermanent and destined to disintegrate while the soul was immortal and imperishable. A second perspective belonged to the Pharisees. The Pharisees believed good souls would pass into a resurrected body. A third perspective belonged to the Sadducees. The Sadducees denied any life to come.

This explanation of the primary perspectives on the afterlife during the time of Jesus and the early church is helpful to understanding thoughts on the afterlife in the New Testament.

Why is the New Testament—unlike the Hebrew Scriptures—filled with thoughts on the afterlife? Because—outside of the Sadducees' perspective—first-century Jews were awash in a consciousness that had begun to assume what Daniel had only begun to imagine: life after death. For this reason, throughout the New Testament we're able to observe evolving thoughts on the afterlife as its authors wrestle with life in Christ within a consciousness that assumed some kind of life after death.

---

5. Josephus, *Antiquities* 18.1.3–5 (Whiston, 572).

CHAPTER 6. AN EVOLUTIONARY AFTERLIFE STORY

Explaining Apocalyptic Jewish Perspective

Besides understanding the three primary perspectives on the afterlife during the life of Jesus, it's important to understand another common Jewish perspective called "apocalyptic Jewish perspective," which rose during the time of Daniel and continued into the time of Jesus.[6] Simply put, apocalyptic Jewish perspective can be described as follows: God's judgment was coming soon, evil would be destroyed, and the good would enter into God's peaceful kingdom here on earth.[7]

Matthew and Mark Thoughts on the Afterlife

In the earliest Gospels—Matthew and Mark—we see an emphasis on apocalyptic Jewish perspective in Jesus' teachings.[8] This apocalyptic emphasis results in the use of apocalyptic judgment language.[9] Although this language has been used by Christians to make conclusions about an afterlife, an honest assessment makes clear that very few afterlife conclusions should be made.

    6. Elledge, *Resurrection of the Dead*; Bremmer, *Rise and Fall*; Ehrman, *Heaven and Hell*; Davies, *Apocalyptic Paul*.

    7. Ehrman, *Heaven and Hell*, 166–67.

    8. The dates for New Testament books throughout this chapter begin by considering Marcus Borg's *Evolution of the Word*, which carefully and eruditely suggests dates aligning with the findings of many biblical scholars today. Matthew was written in the 80s or early 90s. Mark was written around the year 70.

    9. I want to briefly address Jesus' frightening afterlife language referenced in this section and the following sections. For modern readers, Jesus' use of frightening language is, well, frightening! Yet, it's consistent with the tone and nature of apocalyptic literature written around the time of Jesus' life. In this particular literary genre, exaggeration and peril are leveraged as rhetorical tools to startle people and to effect change. About this, it needs to be understood that the effected change is the primary point of this literature, not the circumstances it describes. Besides, the circumstances being described are often expressed through hyperbolic and parabolic literary forms. For this reason, very few conclusions should be made about the afterlife itself. Finally, and most importantly, today, Jesus' frightening words are used to get people to believe certain things so they won't go to hell. However, Jesus' use of frightening language is to motivate people to live ethical and loving lives in *this* world.

PART II. A BIT ON EVOLUTION

Some of the apocalyptic language Jesus uses includes "weeping," "gnashing," "fire," "furnace of fire," "judgment," "day of judgment," and "outer darkness."[10] A few examples:

> Even now the ax is lying at the root of the trees; every tree therefore that does not bear good fruit is cut down and thrown into the *fire*.[11]
>
> I tell you, on the *day of judgment* you will have to give an account for every careless word you utter; for by your words you will be justified, and by your words you will be condemned.[12]
>
> But if that wicked slave says to himself, "My master is delayed," and he begins to beat his fellow slaves, and eats and drinks with drunkards, the master of that slave will come on a day when he does not expect him and at an hour that he does not know. He will cut him in pieces and put him with the hypocrites, where there will be *weeping and gnashing of teeth*.[13]

About these examples, a few observations:

> Jesus explains these outcomes are based on wicked lives.
>
> Other than emphasizing death and destruction, little else can be made of these words.
>
> Jesus uses these words to rouse righteous living here and now.

---

10. Matt 3:10, 12; 5:21–22; 6:30; 7:19; 8:12; 10:15; 11:22–24; 12:36, 41–42; 13:40; 18:8, 9; 22:13; 24:51; 25:30, 41; Mark 9:43, 48–49.
11. Matt 3:10.
12. Matt 12:36–37.
13. Matt 24:48–51.

CHAPTER 6. AN EVOLUTIONARY AFTERLIFE STORY

Another common apocalyptic word Jesus uses is "hell."[14] The Greek word translated as "hell" throughout Matthew and Mark is *gehenna*.[15] However, gehenna isn't some place down in the earth. Instead, gehenna used to be a very real place on the earth. Gehenna was a desecrated valley outside of Jerusalem believed by Jews to be forsaken by God due to pagans sacrificing children there. And so, it became known as a place where corpses were piled up due to wickedness.[16] By the time of Jesus' life, gehenna was well known as a place to burn the bodies of one's enemies.[17]

About this, a few observations:

> For Jesus' audience, hell/gehenna wasn't a place in the earth but on the earth.
>
> To be thrown into hell/gehenna was to be annihilated, not to suffer eternally.
>
> Jesus' use of hell/gehenna was to rouse righteous living here and now.

Turning from these threatening apocalyptic words, Jesus uses encouraging apocalyptic words such as "life" and "treasure."[18] A couple examples:

> Enter through the narrow gate; for the gate is wide and the road is easy that leads to destruction, and there are

---

14. "Hades" is used twice in Matthew (Matt 11:23, 16:18). Only once could its use be thought of as a reference to an afterlife (Matt 11:20–24). However, its use is clearly a picture of destruction, not eternal punishment. Furthermore, the destruction is for those who do not believe in Jesus' miracles, not for those who deny faith in shed blood for the forgiveness of sins.

15. Matt 5:22, 29–30; 10:28; 18:9; 23:15; Mark 9:43–47.

16. 2 Kgs 23:10, Jer 7:29–34.

17. Von Wyrick, "Dynasty That Ruled Jews," 489; Ehrman, *Heaven and Hell*, 156–61.

18. Matt 5:12; 6:1–2, 4–5, 16, 18, 19–21; 7:14; 10:39, 41–42; 12:35, 34; 16:25–26; 18:8–9; 19:16–17, 21; 25:46; Mark 8:35–37; 9:41, 43–45; 10:17, 21, 30, 45.

many who take it. For the gate is narrow and the road is hard that leads to *life*, and there are few who find it.[19]

Jesus, looking at him, loved him and said, "You lack one thing; go, sell what you own, and give the money to the poor, and you will have *treasure* in heaven; then come, follow me."[20]

Similar to Jesus' use of threatening apocalyptic words, the same conclusions can be made about his encouraging apocalyptic words:

These outcomes are based on righteous lives.

The actual meaning of these words is unclear.

Jesus uses these words to encourage righteous living here and now.

Finally, Christians today often refer to an afterlife using the words "resurrection," "heaven," and "eternal." We'll now briefly consider those words.

A future resurrection is referred to just twice in Matthew and Mark.[21] Both uses refer to the same story in which the Sadducees try to outwit Jesus about the idea of a future resurrection in relation to marriage.[22] According to Jesus, in the resurrection, humans will neither marry nor be given in marriage. This passage raises more questions about an afterlife than it answers.

The word "heaven" is used numerous times in Matthew and Mark, but a brief overview of its use results in a confusing array of

---

19. Matt 7:13–14.
20. Mark 10:21.
21. Matt 22, Mark 12.

22. This is a great example of two of the three primary perspectives on the afterlife during the life of Jesus colliding. Here we see the Pharisees' belief in a bodily resurrection being challenged by the Sadducees, who do not believe in a resurrection.

CHAPTER 6. AN EVOLUTIONARY AFTERLIFE STORY

ideas.[23] Jesus says some will be called "least" or "great" in heaven, a person can store up treasures in heaven, not everyone will enter the kingdom of heaven, many will eat with Abraham, Isaac, and Jacob in the kingdom of heaven, only by becoming like a child can a person enter heaven, by selling all possessions a person will have treasure in heaven, a rich person will have a difficult time entering heaven, and heaven and earth will pass away.[24]

About this, a few observations:

> It is impossible to know what exactly heaven is or where it is.
>
> The way in which a person enters heaven is due to becoming like a child, selling all of your possessions, or living righteously.
>
> Rather than being an eternal abode, heaven, like earth, will pass away.

In Matthew and Mark, the word "eternal" is used nine times.[25] It's connected to "life" five times, "fire" two times, and "punishment"

---

23. Matt 3:2, 16–17; 4:17; 5:3, 10, 12, 16, 18–20, 34, 45; 6:1, 9–10, 20; 7:11, 21; 8:11; 10:7, 32; 11:11, 23, 25; 12:50; 13:11, 24, 31, 33, 44, 45, 47, 52; 14:19; 16:1, 17, 19; 18:1, 3, 10, 14, 18–19, 23; 19:12, 14, 21, 23; 20:1, 9, 25; 22:2, 30; 23:9, 13, 22; 24:29–31, 35, 36; 25:1; 26:64; 28:2, 18; Mark 1:10–11; 6:41; 7:34; 8:11; 10:21; 11:10, 25, 30; 12:25; 13:25, 27, 31–32; 14:62; 16:19.

24. Matt 5:19–20, 6:20, 7:21, 8:11, 18:3, 19:21, 19:23, 24:35.

25. The word "eternal" is an English translation of the Greek word αἰώνιός. It can be translated as a long period of time or as a period of time without end (BDAG, s.v. "αἰώνιός"). αἰώνιός comes from the Greek root αἰών, which refers to a long period of time or to a segment of time in history. In light of Matthew and Mark's apocalyptic Jewish perspectives, it's likely that Jesus isn't referring to eternality but to an age of judgment—destruction for the wicked and reward for the righteous. For this reason, some biblical scholars prefer to interpret "eternal life" as "the life of the age to come." This chapter won't further explore the idea of "eternal life" throughout the Gospels. However, it should be noted that John uses the phrase the most—seventeen times. Among John's usages, eternal life is at times a present reality. For example, John 5:24–25: "Very truly, I tell you, anyone who hears my word and believes him who sent me has

PART II. A BIT ON EVOLUTION

and "sin" one time each.[26] About eternal sin, Jesus says, "Whoever blasphemes against the Holy Spirit can never have forgiveness, but is guilty of an *eternal sin*" (Mark 3:29). This is a strange verse, only found in Mark.

About the two uses of eternal fire, Jesus says, "If your hand or your foot causes you to stumble, cut it off and throw it from you; it is better for you to enter life crippled or lame, than to have two hands or two feet and be cast into the *eternal fire*" (Matt 18:8). Then, in Jesus' parable about the sheep and goats, the king says to those who don't care for those in need, "Depart from me, accursed ones, into the *eternal fire* which has been prepared for the devil and his angels" (Matt 25:41). It's in this same parable that the king says those who don't care for the needy will "go away into *eternal punishment*," while those who do care for the needy will enter into "*eternal life*" (Matt 25:46).[27]

This leaves four other uses of the words "eternal life," which are found in the same story, told in Matt 19:16–30 and Mark 10:17–31. In this story, a rich man asks Jesus what he must do to inherit *eternal life*. Jesus responds by telling him to obey the commandments. The rich man tells Jesus he has kept the commandments since he was a boy. Jesus then tells him to go and sell everything he has and to come follow him.

Similar to Jesus' other apocalyptic words we have considered, the same observations can be made:

---

eternal life, and does not come under judgment, but has passed from death to life. Very truly, I tell you, the hour is coming, and is now here, when the dead will hear the voice of the Son of God, and those who hear will live." According to John, to believe in God who sent Jesus results in eternal life—here and now.

26. Matt 18:8; 19:6, 29; 25:41, 46; Mark 3:29; 10:17, 30.

27. Returning to Jesus' use of frightening afterlife language, it's most often found in parabolic and hyperbolic language, which—rhetorically speaking—employ exaggeration and alarm to make a point. Again, notice Jesus' afterlife language is used to motivate people to live ethical and loving lives *in this world*.

CHAPTER 6. AN EVOLUTIONARY AFTERLIFE STORY

These outcomes are based on unrighteous and righteous lives.

The actual meaning of these words is unclear.

Jesus uses these words to encourage righteous living, here and now.

Explaining Non-Apocalyptic Jewish Perspective

As we move to the later Gospels of Luke and John, many of Jesus' apocalyptic Jewish perspectives are repeated.[28] However, a noticeable shift begins to occur in these books, which reflects a non-apocalyptic Jewish perspective. The primary difference between these two perspectives is fairly straightforward. In an apocalyptic Jewish perspective, the emphasis is on God's judgment coming soon, on earth. However, in a non-apocalyptic Jewish perspective, the emphasis shifts to God's judgment taking place somewhere else.[29]

Luke and John Thoughts on the Afterlife

Luke tells two afterlife stories that align with non-apocalyptic Jewish perspective. The first story, found only in Luke, is located in chapter 16. It's often referred to as "The Parable of the Rich Man and Lazarus." In this parable, a righteous poor man named Lazarus is dead but lives on by being carried to Abraham's bosom.[30] A wicked rich man is also dead, but he's suffering in Hades.[31] The wicked rich man in Hades can see the poor man

---

28. Luke was written in the late 80s or early 90s. John was written around the year 90.

29. Ehrman, *Heaven and Hell*, 191–93.

30. The Greek word for "bosom," κολπος, refers to bosom, breast, chest, and the fold of a garment (BDAG, s.v. "κολπος"). "Bosom" throughout the Scriptures is the metaphorical or literal location of intimacy, vulnerability, comfort, and safety (Von Wyrick, "Dynasty That Ruled Jews," 197).

31. In Greek thought, Hades is (a) a proper noun that refers to the Greek

PART II. A BIT ON EVOLUTION

Lazarus at Abraham's side, and he begs for relief. Abraham responds to the wicked rich man telling him the chasm between them is too great, and besides, while on earth he had ease while Lazarus had hardship. For this reason, Abraham explains Lazarus is now comforted while the rich man is tormented.

According to this story,

> the place of Hades seems to be somewhere down in the earth while Abraham's bosom seems to be up, somewhere,
>
> despite being in different places, the wicked rich man can see and talk to Abraham,
>
> the wicked rich man is said to be in Hades because on earth, he was rich and didn't care for the poor,
>
> and the poor man Lazarus is said to be in Abraham's bosom because on earth, he suffered.

In a second story found only in Luke, Jesus is crucified between two criminals. One criminal mocks Jesus but the other criminal defends him. He then asks Jesus to remember him, to which Jesus replies, "I tell you the truth, today you will be with me in paradise."[32]

According to this story,

> a crucified criminal will go to paradise because he defends Jesus and asks to be remembered by him,
>
> and this crucified criminal will go to paradise immediately after death.

---

god of the netherworld and (b) a netherworld for the dead (BDAG, s.v. "ᾅδης")

32. Luke 23:43. Paradise, from the Greek word παραδεισος, can refer to the garden of Eden or to a transcendent place of blessedness (BDAG, s.v. "παραδεισος").

CHAPTER 6. AN EVOLUTIONARY AFTERLIFE STORY

Although John doesn't contain either of these stories from Luke, it does contain a story that reflects non-apocalyptic Jewish perspective. At the end of John 13, Jesus tells his disciples he will only be with them a little longer. Peter asks, "Where are you going?" Jesus replies, "Where I am going, you cannot follow me now; but you will follow afterward" (verse 36). Then, in the beginning of John 14, Jesus says,

> Do not let your hearts be troubled. Believe in God, believe also in me. In my Father's house there are many dwelling places. If it were not so, would I have told you that I go to prepare a place for you? And if I go and prepare a place for you, I will come again and will take you to myself, so that where I am, there you may be also. And you know the way to the place where I am going.[33]

According to this story,

> the disciples are to believe in God and in Jesus,
>
> the Father's house has many dwelling places,
>
> Jesus is going to prepare a place for his disciples,
>
> Jesus will return to take his disciples with him to the place he is preparing,
>
> and it's unclear when Jesus will return to take his disciples with him.[34]

While this story inches closer toward what many Christians think about the afterlife today, it's still strikingly different. The disciples are merely told to believe in God and in Jesus, which results in Jesus promising he will come to take them away to his Father's house.[35] Whatever is to be made of "believe in God, believe also in

---

33. John 14:1–4.

34. A fair reading of the text suggests Jesus will return to retrieve his disciples while they are still alive.

35. This generic use of the concept of "belief" is consistent throughout

PART II. A BIT ON EVOLUTION

me," it doesn't have anything to do with belief in Jesus' shed blood on a cross for the forgiveness of sins. Jesus has yet to be crucified.

These examples from Luke and John reveal similarity and evolution in Jesus' words about the afterlife in Matthew and Mark. The similarity is that Jesus uses the afterlife to rouse righteous living in this life, as we observed in the parable of the rich man and Lazarus, from Luke 16. The evolution is that Jesus tells different people they will end up in different places for different reasons. In Luke 16, the rich man goes to Hades because he was rich and had ease in this life; Lazarus goes to Abraham's bosom because he was poor and suffered in this life. In Luke 23, Jesus tells the criminal he will be in paradise today for defending him while on the cross. In John 14, Jesus tells the disciples he will return to take them with him to the place he is preparing for believing in God and in him.

Paul Thoughts on the Afterlife

This brings us to the evolution of thought on the afterlife in the writings of Paul. It's through Paul that the afterlife becomes

---

John's Gospel in phrases like, "His disciples believed in him" (John 2:11); "They believed in the scripture" (John 2:22); "The man believed the word that Jesus spoke" (John 4:50); "Then Jesus said to the Jews who had believed in him, 'If you continue in my word, you are truly my disciples'" (John 8:31); "He said, 'Lord, I believe.' And he worshiped him" (John 9:38); "Many of the Jews therefore, who had come with Mary and had seen what Jesus did, believed in him" (John 11:45); "Believe me that I am in the Father and the Father is in me; but if you do not, then believe me because of the works themselves" (John 14:11); "As you, Father, are in me and I am in you, may they also be in us, so that the world may believe that you have sent me" (John 17:21); "But these are written so that you may come to believe that Jesus is the Messiah, the Son of God, and that through believing you may have life in his name" (John 20:31). This broad range of examples from the Gospel of John demonstrates the kind of belief that Jesus is seeking, which reflects the general meaning of the Greek word for "believe," πιστεύω. It is defined as, "Considering something or someone to be true and worthy of trust; to entrust oneself to an entity in complete confidence" (BDAG, s.v. "πιστεύω"). Rather than demanding creedal belief, Jesus consistently invites his followers to trust in him and in his way of life, which is loving, just, and ethical throughout the Gospels.

CHAPTER 6. AN EVOLUTIONARY AFTERLIFE STORY

associated with Jesus' death on a cross. Through the interpretive lens of accommodation, this makes sense. Trained as a Pharisee, Paul would have been a staunch believer in a bodily resurrection. He would have also been awash in Jewish temple theology and the need of blood sacrifice for the forgiveness of sins. As a converted Pharisee and follower of Jesus, a chronological look at Paul's letters reveals an evolution of thought on the afterlife as he attempts to make meaningful connections between Jesus' death and a bodily resurrection.

Continuing in my attempt at brevity, Paul's earliest letter—1 Thessalonians—explains a three-tiered world in which there are those who are asleep in the earth, those who live on the earth, and Jesus who will one day descend from heaven.[36] According to Paul, those who believe Jesus died and rose again will be caught up in the clouds with the Lord, but the wicked will face destruction.[37]

In a later letter by Paul—1 Corinthians—he begins to work out a bodily resurrection.[38] In this stage of Paul's thoughts on an afterlife, bodily resurrection is reserved for heavenly bodies only. For according to Paul, all other dominions and authorities will be destroyed.[39]

In a later letter by Paul—2 Corinthians—he begins to work out a judgment before Christ.[40] In this stage of Paul's thoughts on an afterlife, every person will receive their recompense.[41] However, recompense is not explained.

---

36. 1 Thessalonians was written around the year 50.
37. 1 Thess 4:13–18, 5:3.
38. 1 Corinthians was written around the year 53 or 54.
39. 1 Cor 15:24, 40–41.
40. 2 Corinthians was written around the late 50s.
41. 2 Cor 5:1–4, 10.

Finally, in yet a later letter—Romans—Paul explains there will be a day of judgment for every person based on deeds.[42] Those who are justified by Jesus' blood will be saved from God's wrath; those who are not justified by Jesus' blood will experience God's wrath.[43]

Summary

Before getting to Revelation, I want to pause to highlight a clearly observable evolution of the afterlife—based on context and human consciousness—throughout the Bible.

As we have observed, thoughts on the afterlife begin in Daniel, evolve in the Gospels, and continue to evolve throughout Paul's letters.

In Daniel, we observe the genesis of thought on the afterlife, which grows up out of the human longing for justice. And so, Daniel explains,

> many people who sleep in the dust will rise,
>
> some will rise to everlasting contempt,
>
> and some will rise to everlasting life.

In the early Gospels—Matthew and Mark—we observe an evolution of thought on the afterlife, which grows up out of a Jewish apocalyptic perspective. And so, Matthew and Mark explain,

> God's judgment is coming soon,
>
> evil will be destroyed,
>
> and the good will enter into God's peaceful kingdom here on earth.

---

42. Romans was written around the year 58.
43. Rom 2:5–10, 5:9, 9:22.

CHAPTER 6. AN EVOLUTIONARY AFTERLIFE STORY

In the later Gospels—Luke and John—we observe an evolution of thought on the afterlife, which grows up out of a non-apocalyptic Jewish perspective. And so, Luke and John explain,

> the poor Lazarus will go to Abraham's bosom,
>
> the rich man will go to Hades,
>
> the criminal who defends Jesus will go to paradise, immediately after death,
>
> and the disciples who believe in God and in Jesus will be taken to the Father's house.

In Paul, we observe yet more evolution of thought on the afterlife, which grows up out of his pharisaical perspective and temple theology paradigm. And so, Paul emphasizes the need for trust in Jesus' shed blood for the forgiveness of sins to be saved, while slowly working out a theology on the afterlife that progresses.

> From:
>
> The alive in Christ will rise to meet Jesus in the clouds, while those outside of Christ are destroyed.
>
> To:
>
> Those in Christ will receive heavenly bodies, while those outside of Christ are destroyed.
>
> To:
>
> Every person will stand judgment before Christ and receive their recompense.
>
> To:
>
> A day of judgment based on deeds will occur for every person.

PART II. A BIT ON EVOLUTION

Revelation Thoughts on the Afterlife

With this summary in mind, the Bible's evolution on the afterlife concludes in the final three chapters of Revelation.[44] These chapters are very different from the afterlife we traced through the Gospels and writings of Paul. In a final attempt at brevity, the last three chapters of Revelation provide a cosmic picture of an afterlife during which

> evil is finally and decisively destroyed,[45]
>
> the dead are judged,[46]
>
> heaven descends and weds with earth,[47]
>
> and all is at peace because satan, the beast, the false prophet, death, and Hades are all thrown into what is called "the lake of fire"[48]—about which, much debate occurs.[49]

Evolution of Thoughts on the Afterlife in Church History

Based on this overview, it's easy to appreciate how confusing it must have been for the early church to know what to think about the afterlife. Biblically speaking, the afterlife isn't nearly as clear or developed as many Christians think. This is due to the fact that the afterlife story many Christians tell today isn't the result of biblical studies but church tradition.

---

44. Revelation was written around the 90s.
45. Rev 20:7–9.
46. Rev 20:11–13
47. Rev 21:1–2.
48. Rev 20:10, 14.
49. Are these apocalyptic texts to be read literally or figuratively? What is the nature of fire? Is it annihilation, purgation, or torment? Since satan, the beast, the false prophet, death, and Hades are thrown into the lake of fire, what is it, where is it, what exactly happens in it, and who is in control of it? Etc.

CHAPTER 6. AN EVOLUTIONARY AFTERLIFE STORY

I'd like to say that again:

> The afterlife story many Christians tell today isn't the result of biblical studies but church tradition.

Let me briefly explain why. Because the Bible's thoughts on the afterlife lack clarity and evolve, the early church wrestled with what to think about life after death. This wrestling included thoughts on the interim stage between death and resurrection, whether the resurrection included a physical body or just a soul, and whether or not a person could be saved postmortem.

As I shared at the beginning of this chapter, by the third century, church father Tertullian of Carthage explained an afterlife that is vastly different from the one many Christians believe in today. This means that contemporary Christian thought on the afterlife has been deeply shaped by contexts and stages of human consciousness, post–Tertullian of Carthage. And this means that contemporary Christian thought on the afterlife has been deeply shaped by contexts and stages of human consciousness that existed within

> the medieval church,
> the Protestant church,
> and the United States of America church.

To better understand these perspectives, think about Dante's *Inferno* from the fourteenth century, or that horrifying sermon by Jonathan Edwards from the eighteenth century titled "Sinners in the Hands of an Angry God," or the literally interpreted apocalyptic notions proposed by John Darby in the nineteenth century, which became core facets to thought on the afterlife within Christian Fundamentalism.

PART II. A BIT ON EVOLUTION

My point—while provocative for those who think their thoughts on the afterlife life go back to the early church or to the Bible or to the life of Jesus—is reasonable and defendable:

> Contemporary Christian thought on the afterlife is not, ultimately, biblical.

Instead, it's the result of an evolution of thought shaped by historical contexts and stages of human consciousness spanning millennia.

The Table This Story Sets

This brief overview is crucial to telling a more honest afterlife story, which is capable of setting a table with loving features.

> *One feature of the table this afterlife story sets is humility.*

We Christians do not know exactly what will happen after we die. No one can point to a verse or to a moment in church history to articulate a clear and straightforward perspective on the afterlife. It doesn't exist. For this reason, rather than thinking we need to wholeheartedly affirm without reservation some kind of doctrine on the afterlife to be Christian, it would be so much more honest to simply say Christian thought on the afterlife is vast, and it's gone through numerous evolutions. More so, these numerous evolutions have been deeply shaped by historical contexts and stages of human consciousness.

> *A second feature of the table this afterlife story sets is an openness to dialogue and ongoing evolution.*

This point isn't radical. It's merely an acceptance of what is. From the very beginning, historical contexts and stages of human

CHAPTER 6. AN EVOLUTIONARY AFTERLIFE STORY

consciousness have given shape to an evolution of thought on the afterlife, in the Bible and throughout church history.

This honest assessment makes me want to ask, why stop now? Why allow fourteenth-, eighteenth-, and nineteenth-century contexts and stages of consciousness to be the final word on what we think about the afterlife? What might this twenty-first-century context and stage of consciousness contribute to our thoughts on the afterlife? For example, what might physics, subatomic theory, and quantum entanglement have to teach us about the afterlife, especially in light of our doctrine on the Trinity—the inter-relationality of Ultimate Reality itself? Based on the church's evolution of thought on the afterlife, that's worth exploring.[50]

> *A third feature of the table this afterlife story sets is a commitment to justice when we tell stories about the afterlife.*

Justice is where it all began. Thoughts on the afterlife grew up out of Daniel's longing for justice. For this reason, justice should ground the stories of the afterlife we tell. And because the notion of justice evolves along with human consciousness, Christians should be the first to let go of stories about an afterlife that can no longer be considered just—for example, a story explaining the majority of humans will be eternally tormented in hell for not believing in God's need for shed blood to forgive sins. That's an old, archaic, and violent—which is to say, unjust—perspective on both God and the afterlife. We must let unjust ways of thinking go when it comes to our afterlife stories.

> *A fourth feature of the table this afterlife story sets is goodness for today.*

---

50. Some authors to consider reading who are wrestling with theology in light of post-Newtonian science include Ilea Delio, Peter Russell, and John Polkinghorne.

PART II. A BIT ON EVOLUTION

That's one thing Daniel, the Gospels, and Paul all have in common in their perspectives on the afterlife: how we live today matters. That's why each of them says something about rewards and punishment in the life to come based on how humans live in this life, here and now. Unfortunately, for many people today the idea of an afterlife has come to mean this world is heading to hell in a handbasket, and so doing good—caring for this planet, improving systems, and working out a salvation dealing with real predicaments—is often deemed unnecessary. Tragically, that's a complete misunderstanding and misappropriation of Christianity's afterlife story, which from the beginning was meant to rouse goodness, here and now.

Here and now:

> An evolving afterlife story that sparks humility because we don't know exactly what will happen after death.

Here and now:

> An evolving afterlife story that considers historical contexts and stages of human consciousness resulting in an openness to dialogue and ongoing evolution regarding what happens after we die.

Here and now:

> An evolving afterlife story shaped by contemporary notions of justice to ensure that our afterlife storytelling isn't archaic or violent.

Here and now:

> An evolving afterlife story that's good for today—bettering this planet, improving systems, and working out a salvation dealing with real life predicaments.

Part III. A Bit on Religious Tradition

Before the term "Christian," there was simply the historical Jesus known as "Jesus, son of Joseph" and "Jesus of Nazareth." Over the course of a few short years, this Jesus accrued followers known as "disciples." After his crucifixion and before Saul's conversion to Paul, Jesus' disciples were identified as "followers of the way."[1] Just a couple chapters later, these disciples were called "Christians" for the first time.[2]

The word "Christian" is derived from the Greek word "Christ," which means "the anointed one." Throughout the Gospels, Jesus is often referred to as "Jesus Christ." In Greek literature, it was common to add the suffix *-ianos* after a leader's name. In this way, Christ followers came to be called "Christians" after Jesus' death.

With this context in mind, Jewish Christians spread their faith throughout the Roman province of Judea, the converted Christian Paul spread his faith throughout the gentile provinces in the Roman Empire, and by the fourth century, Christianity became the official religion of the Roman Empire. According to the

---

1. Acts 9:2.
2. Acts 11:26.

PART III. A BIT ON RELIGIOUS TRADITION

majority of statistics on religion today, around 2.4 billion people identify as Christian.[3]

Question: What is Christianity?

Answer: Christianity is a religion.

Religion.

Religion is derived from the Latin *religio*, meaning reverence for the gods, holiness, a system of belief.

Religio is derived from the Latin *religare*, re = back, and *ligare* = to bind. It's from this word that we get the English word, "ligament(s)."[4]

Question: What is Christianity?

Answer: Christianity is a tradition.

Tradition.

Tradition is derived from the Latin *traditio*, meaning delivery of or the action of handing over stories, beliefs, and customs.

Question: What is Christianity?

Answer: Christianity is a religious tradition.

Religious Tradition.

---

3. World Population Review, "Most Christian Countries"; Hackett et al., Christian Population Change"; Zurlo et al., "World Christianity 2025."
4. Lewis and Short, *Latin Dictionary*, s.v. "religio."

PART III. A BIT ON RELIGIOUS TRADITION

Religious tradition is a system for reverence, holiness, and belief that binds people together and is passed on from one generation to the next through stories, beliefs, and customs.

> Stories,
>> beliefs,
>>> and customs.
>
> Like ligaments,
>> can hold us together.

The closing chapter of this book explores the flourishing that can be nurtured by being involved in an evolving religious tradition intent on discerning and embodying good.

Chapter 7. **Held Together by Christian Life**

Many people today think religion is a thing of the past and should remain there. I'm in complete agreement, *if*. If the religion is incoherent, violent, and animated by fear, I agree it has no place in today's society. That kind of religion is unhelpful and not needed. However, I'm not convinced this makes religion unnecessary.

As far back as we know, humans have had their religions. As far back as we know, humans have gathered to tell stories, pray prayers, sing songs, celebrate feasts, progress through rites of passage, and live out their lives in communities before their gods.

Why?

Could it be possible that religion functions to uniquely meet some of our human needs that no other system or discipline has, so far, been capable of meeting? I have come to think so, and what follows are some of my primary reasons.

Fundamental Questions

At one time or another, every human asks, "Who am I?" "What am I?" "Why am I here?" "What is important?" "What is the good life?"

PART III. A BIT ON RELIGIOUS TRADITION

What are we to do about these fundamental questions?

The most honest answer is that we cannot fully or perfectly answer them. No science, philosophy, or religion can claim perfect knowledge related to these fundamental questions.

Freed from the hubris of perfect answers to fundamental questions, we're invited into the age-old human journey of pursuing, pondering, and wrestling with the meaning of life.

The meaning of *life*.

Where do we even begin?

According to Iain McGilchrist, the pursuit of the meaning of life is a shared responsibility among science, philosophy, and religion.[1] McGilchrist explains, "Science is not just a technique, but, rightly conceived, the groundwork for illuminating something lying beyond itself." However, that which is lying beyond itself is beyond science. For this reason, McGilchrist writes, "This is why philosophy needs science, and science needs philosophy."[2] However, even philosophy has its limits when attempting to explain that which is lying beyond itself. And so, McGilchrist encourages the use of religious language to help in our pursuit of that which is lying beyond itself, explaining, "The ordinary name for that which is the logical ground of everything else is God."[3] According to McGilchrist, invoking God ensures we don't lose sight of life's deepest enigmas and mysteries.

Enigmas and mysteries.

---

1. Iain McGilchrist is one of today's brightest intellectuals. He's a psychiatrist, neuroscience researcher, philosopher, and literary scholar, among other things.
2. McGilchrist, *Matter with Things*, 2:1203.
3. McGilchrist, *Matter with Things*, 2:1203.

CHAPTER 7. HELD TOGETHER BY CHRISTIAN LIFE

Now we're getting somewhere.

Participating in a Christian life encourages us to thoughtfully wrestle, in community with others, with the great enigmas and mysteries of existence. Of course, Christianity has a history of attempting to force these enigmas and mysteries into doctrines to be believed, or else. But that just kills the mystery.

Rather than the affirmation of Christian doctrine, I find wrestling with Christian mysteries to be invigorating and wonderfully helpful as I consider fundamental questions about life. For example:

> God—the mystery of Ultimate Reality?
>
> Incarnation—the mystery of God in all of materiality?
>
> Atonement—the mystery of reconciling estrangement?
>
> Resurrection—the mystery of life over death?
>
> And Trinity-the mystery of Ultimate Reality's inter-relationality?

Encouraged by Christian life to abide within these mysteries and to intentionally explore their meaning, I find my life is better off. I find there's more curiosity, wonder, and with great humility, conviction, which helps me to thoughtfully explore the fundamental questions we all ask.

Spirituality

The word "spiritual" refers to the nonmaterial and nonphysical aspects of our human existence—for example, awe, wonder, gratitude, mercy, forgiveness, and the development of character and convictions. These spiritual aspects of human existence are significant. But they need ongoing attention and thought to become a meaningful part of our humanity. As Arthur Brooks explains, "Spiritual experiences have a deep scientific basis to them, and

PART III. A BIT ON RELIGIOUS TRADITION

transcendental experiences provide us with important information about life we cannot get in any other way. Getting these experiences, however, takes effort and commitment."[4]

Unfortunately, the nurturing of spirituality is neglected in many, if not most, of the domains where we live out our lives. As a necessary counterbalance to this aperture, religious traditions exist. I find participating in a Christian life accentuates spirituality, encouraging me to pay attention to nonmaterial and nonphysical aspects of my being human:

>Awe,
>>wonder,
>>>gratitude,
>>>>mercy,
>>>>>forgiveness,
>>>>>>character,
>>>>>>>and convictions?

Yes, please.

Subversive Embodiment

Many of us look at the world today and feel great concern and little hope. We wonder, "What can I possibly do?" We can, of course, give time and money to political parties, candidates, and organizations we believe in. We can also march, and scream, and vote. But then what? What can we *do*? What can we meaningfully do here, now, in our lives?

Let's begin with what we can't do:

Immediately extricate misogyny and homophobia.

---

4. Brooks and Winfrey, *Build the Life You Want*, 178.

CHAPTER 7. HELD TOGETHER BY CHRISTIAN LIFE

Immediately disentangle racism.

Immediately alter policies harming climate care, humane treatment of undocumented citizens, and a social safety net for the most vulnerable.

Immediately topple violent and dominion politics and religion.

Here's what we can do:

Participate in a community that celebrates the full inclusion of women and LGBTQIA+ people.

Participate in a community that commits itself to anti-racism.

Participate in a community that treasures the interrelationality of all things.

Participate in a community that wholeheartedly declares a gospel that is, in all honesty, good—especially for the most vulnerable.

Truly good Christian communities are subversive embodiments of the world we want. Our participation in them makes that world manifest, here and now. By experiencing that world on a regular basis, our expectations for a better world solidify and grow. The world we want is possible.

Filled with hope,
> weariness and lethargy are replaced by conviction and vitality.

Filled with hope,
> we become an unceasing force for good.

Filled with hope,
> we will not rest until the kingdom of God—peace on earth—is made manifest.

PART III. A BIT ON RELIGIOUS TRADITION

The Way

Today, we live in a postmodern world. Postmodernism is a reaction against modernism's certainty. In contrast to modernism's emphasis on certain logic, rationality, and universality of meaning, postmodernism emphasizes complexity, contradiction, and layers of meaning. I'm very much a product of postmodernism, and I have benefited from its criticism of thoughts and structures. However, like any other cultural development, postmodernism has its deficits. A primary deficit is the void its criticism creates.

As an example, consider these two words: the way. Postmodernism immediately snickers at the absurdity. The way? No way! There are many ways. It's true. A person can live a hundred different ways. However, is every way good? Does every way lead to flourishing? And by the way, who gets to determine what's good or flourishing? We now find ourselves in the existential quagmire of postmodernism.

It's here I find relief in a Christian life. Not as a means to answering all of my questions or to replacing my uncertainty with absolute certainty. Rather, as a way to point me toward . . . The Way.

> A Christian way to The Way—
>
> > Observed through a good Bible story demonstrating humankind's ability to grow up into the wisdom of love through life, death, and resurrection, again and again.
>
> A Christian way to The Way—
>
> > Named through a good gospel story declaring freedom, healing, release, and Divine favor for every person.

CHAPTER 7. HELD TOGETHER BY CHRISTIAN LIFE

A Christian way to The Way—

> Encouraged through a good salvation story bringing an end to every human predicament.

A Christian way to The Way—

> Experienced through an evolutionary atonement story nurturing the reconciliation of everything that's alienated.

A Christian way to The Way—

> Provoked through an evolutionary afterlife story insisting on justice, ethics, and love—here, now, today.

> May Christian life
> > as a religious tradition
> Hold us together in the way
> > of Love.

> May truly good
> > Christian stories
> Set truly loving
> > Christian tables
> That nurture the flourishing
> > of all things.

> May it be so
> > Amen, amen.

Bibliography

Abelard, Peter. *Ethical Writings: Ethics and Dialogue Between a Philosopher, a Jew, and a Christian.* Translated by Paul Vincent Spade. Indianapolis: Hackett, 1995.
Allen, Kelly-Ann, et al. "Belonging: A Review of Conceptual Issues, an Integrative Framework, and Directions for Future Research." *Australian Journal of Psychology* 73 (2021) 87–102. Doi: 10.1080/00049530.2021.1883409.
Allert, Craig D. *A High View of Scripture?* Grand Rapids: Baker Academic, 2007.
Allison, Dale C. *The Resurrection of Jesus: Apologetics, Polemics, History.* New York: Bloomsbury, 2021.
Anderson, Gary A. *Sin: A History.* New Haven: Yale University Press, 2009.
Anselm of Canterbury. *The Major Works.* Edited by Brian Davies and G. R. Evans. Oxford: Oxford University Press, 2008.
Athanasius. *Festal Letter.* Translated by Archibald Robertson. In vol. 4 of *The Nicene and Post-Nicene Fathers*, 2nd ser. Edited by Philip Schaff. Peabody: Hendrickson, 2004.
Augustine. *City of God.* Translated by Marcus Dods. In vol 2 of *The Nicene and Post-Nicene Fathers*, 1st ser. Edited by Philip Schaff. Peabody: Hendrickson, 2004.
———, *On Christian Doctrine.* Translated by J. F. Shaw. In vol. 2 of *The Nicene and Post-Nicene Fathers*, 1st ser. Edited by Philip Schaff. Peabody: Hendrickson, 2004.
Aulén, Gustaf. *Christus Victor.* Translated by A. G. Hebert. Eugene, OR: Wipf & Stock, 2003.
Barbour, Ian. *When Science Meets Religion.* New York: HarperOne, 2000.
Barth, Karl. *Church Dogmatics. 1/2: The Doctrine of the Word of God.* Edited by G. W. Bromily and T. F. Torrance. Translated by G. T. Thomson and Harold Knight. Peabody: Hendrickson, 2010.
Barton, John. *A History of the Bible.* London: Viking, 2019.
Bauckman, Richard. *Jesus and the Eyewitnesses: The Gospels as Eyewitness Testimony.* Grand Rapids: Eerdmans, 2006.

BIBLIOGRAPHY

Bauer, Walter. *A Greek-English Lexicon of the New Testament and other Early Christian Literature*. 3rd ed. Revised and edited by Frederick William Danker. Chicago: University of Chicago Press, 2001.

Baumgartner, Walter, and Ludwig Koehler. *The Hebrew and Aramaic Lexicon of the Old Testament*. Translated by M. E. J. Richardson in collaboration with G. J. Jongeling-Vos and L. J. De Regt. Leiden: Brill, 2000.

Beck, Don Edward, and Christopher C. Cowan. *Spiral Dynamics: Mastering Values, Leadership, and Change*. Malden, MA: Blackwell, 2006.

Beilby, James K., and Paul R. Eddy, eds. *The Historical Jesus: Five Views*. Downers Grove, IL: IVP Academic, 2009.

———, eds. *The Nature of the Atonement: Four Views*. Downers Grove, IL: IVP Academic, 2006.

Bell, Rob. *What Is the Bible?* New York: HarperOne, 2017.

Benin, Stephen D. *The Footprints of God: Divine Accommodation in Jewish and Christian Thought*. Albany: State University of New York Press, 1993.

Bibelhaus Erlebnis Museum. "Calendar Inscription from Priene." https://www.bibelhaus-frankfurt.de/en/bimumag/the-special-object/calendar-inscription-from-priene.

Bonhoeffer, Deitrich. *The Cost of Discipleship*. Translated by R. H. Fuller. Revised by Irmgard Booth. New York: Simon & Schuster, 1995.

———. *Reflections on the Bible: Human Word and Word of God*. Translated by M. E. Boring. Peabody: Hendrickson, 2004.

Borg, Marcus. *Evolution of the Word*. New York: HarperOne, 2012.

———. *The Heart of Christianity*. New York: HarperCollins, 2003.

Bremmer, Jan N. *The Rise and Fall of the Afterlife*. Routledge: New York, 2002.

Brettler, Marc Zvi, and Amy-Jill Levine. *The Bible With and Without Jesus*. Grand Rapids: HarperOne, 2020.

Brooks, Arthur, and Oprah Winfrey. *Build the Life You Want*. New York: Penguin, 2023.

Brown, William P. *Engaging Biblical Authority*. Louisville: Westminster John Knox, 2007.

Burnfield, David. *Patristic Universalism: An Alternative to the Traditional View of Divine Judgment*. Boca Raton, FL: Universal, 2013.

Campbell, Joseph. *The Masks of God*. New York: Random House, 1991.

———. *Pathways to Bliss*. Novato, CA: New World Library, 2004.

———. *The Power of Myth*. New York: Random House, 1988.

Capon, Robert Farrar. *Kingdom, Grace, Judgment*. Grand Rapids: Eerdmans, 1989.

Carroll, James. *Constantine's Sword: The Church and the Jews*. Boston: Houghton Mifflin, 2001.

Chang, Kai-Hsuan. *The Impact of Bodily Experience on Paul's Resurrection Theology*. New York: T. & T. Clark, 2023.

Chesterton, G. K. *Orthodoxy*. New York: Simon & Brown, 2010.

Childs, Brevard. *Introduction to the Old Testament as Scripture*. Philadelphia: Fortress, 1979.

BIBLIOGRAPHY

Chilton, Bruce, et al. *The Cambridge Companion to the Bible*. 2nd ed. New York: Cambridge University Press, 2008.
Clasby, Nancy Tenfelde. *God, the Bible, and Human Consciousness*. New York: Palgrave Macmillan, 2008.
Cone, James H. *The Cross and the Lynching Tree*. New York: Orbis, 2013.
Couchmen, Judith. *The Mystery of the Cross: Bringing Ancient Christian Images to Life*. Downers Grove, IL: InterVarsity, 2009.
Crossan, John Dominic. *God and Empire*. New York: HarperOne, 2007.
Crossan, John Dominic, and Marcus Borg. *The Last Week*. New York: HarperOne, 2006.
Dalley, Stephanie. *Myths from Mesopotamia: Creation, the Flood, Gilgamesh, and Others*. Oxford: Oxford University Press, 2008.
Davies, Jamie. *The Apocalyptic Paul: Retrospect and Prospect*. Eugene, OR: Cascade, 2022.
Dawkins, Richard. *Outgrowing God*. New York: Random House, 2019.
Delio, Ilia. *From Teilhard to Omega*. New York: Orbis, 2014.
———. *Making All Things New*. New York: Orbis, 2020.
———. *The Unbearable Wholeness of Being*. New York: Orbis, 2013.
Dunn, James D. G. *Romans 1-8*. Word Biblical Commentary 38a. Nashville: Thomas Nelson, 1988.
Ehrman, Bart D. *The Bible: A Historical and Literary Introduction*. 2nd ed. New York: Oxford University Press, 2018.
———. *Heaven and Hell*. New York: Simon & Schuster, 2020.
———. *Journey to Heaven and Hell*. New Haven: Yale University Press, 2022.
Einstein, Albert. *Einstein on Cosmic Religion and Other Opinions and Aphorisms*. New York: Dover, 2009.
Elledge, C. D. *Resurrection of the Dead in Early Judaism, 200 BCE-CE 200*. New York: Oxford University Press, 2017.
Enns, Peter. *The Evolution of Adam: What the Bible Does and Doesn't Say About Human Origins*. Grand Rapids: Brazos, 2012.
———. *How the Bible Actually Works*. New York: HarperOne, 2019.
Fitzgerald, Frances. *The Evangelicals*. New York: Simon & Schuster, 2017.
Flower, Harriet I. *Empire and Religion in the Roman World*. New York: Cambridge University Press, 2023.
Flusser, David. *Jesus*. Jerusalem: Magnes, 1998.
Fox, Matthew. *Original Blessing*. New York: Jeremy P. Tarcher / Putnam, 2000.
Garrett, Stephen M., and J. Merrick. *Five Views on Biblical Inerrancy*. Grand Rapids: Zondervan, 2001.
Gorman, Michael J. *Scripture: An Ecumenical Introduction to the Bible and Its Interpretation*. Grand Rapids: Baker Academic, 2005.
Greenblatt, Stephen. *The Rise and Fall of Adam and Eve*. New York: Norton, 2017.
Gregory of Nazianzen. *The Fifth Theological Oration*. Translated by Charles Gordon Browne and James Edward Swallow. In vol. 7 of *The Nicene and Post-Nicene Fathers*, 2nd ser. Edited by Philip Schaff. Peabody: Hendrickson, 1994.

BIBLIOGRAPHY

Gregory the Great. *Morals on the Book of Job*. 3 vols. Translated by John Henry Parker et al. London: Veritatis Splendor, 1884.

Gundry, Stanley N., and Preston Sprinkle. *Four Views on Hell*. Grand Rapids: Zondervan, 2016.

Hackett, Conrad, et al. "Christian Population Change." Pew Research Center, June 9, 2025. https://www.pewresearch.org/religion/2025/06/09/christian-population-change/.

Hanson, J. W. *Universalism: The Prevailing Doctrine of the Christian Church During Its First Five Hundred Years*. Boston: Universalist, 2012.

Hauerwas, Stanley. *The Peaceable Kingdom*. Notre Dame: University of Notre Dame, 1993.

———. *Vision and Virtue*. Notre Dame: University of Notre Dame, 1974.

Hays, Richard B., and Christopher B. Hays. *The Widening of God's Mercy*. New Haven: Yale University Press, 2024.

Hengel, Martin. *Crucifixion*. Philadelphia: Fortress, 1977.

Horrell, David G. *The Making of Christian Morality*. Grand Rapids: Eerdmans, 2019.

Irenaeus. *Against Heresies*. Translated by Alexander Roberts and W. H. Rambaut. In vol. 1 of *The Ante-Nicene Fathers*. Edited by Alexander Roberts and James Donaldson. Peabody: Hendrickson, 2004.

James, William. *The Varieties of Religious Experiences*. New York: Penguin, 1982.

Jipp, Joshua W. *Pauline Theology as a Way of Life*. Grand Rapids: Baker Academic, 2023.

Johnson, Luke Timothy. *Reading Romans: A Literary and Theological Commentary*. New York: Crossroad, 1997.

Josephus, Flavius. *The Antiquities of the Jews*. In *The Complete Works*, translated by William Whiston. Nashville: Thomas Nelson, 1998.

Kim, Young Richard, ed. *The Cambridge Companion to the Council of Nicaea*. Cambridge: Cambridge University Press, 2021.

King, Thomas M. *Teilhard's Mysticism of Knowing*. New York: Seabury, 1981.

Kirk, J. R. Daniel. *Unlocking Romans: Resurrection and the Justification of God*. Grand Rapids: Eerdmans, 2008.

Kugel, James L. *The Bible as It Was*. London: Harvard University Press, 1998.

Lewis, Charlton T., and Charles Short, eds. *A Latin Dictionary*. London: Clarendon, 1879.

Lewis, C. S. *Narnia, Cambridge, and Joy 1950–1963*. Vol. 3 of *The Collected Letters of C. S. Lewis*, edited by Walter Hoper. HarperCollins, e-books, 2009.

Lincoln, Andrew T. *Born a Virgin?* Grand Rapids: Eerdmans, 2013.

Longenecker, Bruce W. *The New Cambridge Companion to St. Paul*. New York: Cambridge University Press, 2020.

Mack, Burton L. *The Lost Gospel: The Book of Q and Christian Origins*. New York: HarperOne, 1993.

BIBLIOGRAPHY

McCulloch, Diarmaid. *Christianity: The First Three Thousand Years*. New York: Viking, 2009.

McGilchrist, Iain. *The Matter with Things: Our Brains, Our Delusions, and the Unmaking of the World*. 2 vols. London: Perspectiva, 2021.

McKnight, Scot, and Dennis R. Venema. *Adam and the Genome*. Grand Rapids: Brazos, 2017.

Miles-Yepez, Netanel, ed. *The Common Heart*. New York: Lantern, 2006.

Mobley, Gregory, and T. J. Wray. *The Birth of Satan: Tracing the Devil's Biblical Roots*. New York: Palgrave, 2005.

Moltmann, Jürgen. *Jesus Christ for Today's World*. Translated by Margaret Kohl. Minneapolis: Fortress, 1994.

Moo, Douglas J. *The Epistle to the Romans*. New International Commentary on the New Testament. Grand Rapids: Eerdmans, 1996.

Morgan, Christopher W., and Robert A. Peterson. *Fallen: A Theology of Sin*. Wheaton, IL: Crossway, 2013.

Morgan, Teresa. *Trust in Atonement*. Grand Rapids: Eerdmans, 2024.

Osborn, Ronald E. *Death Before the Fall*. Downers Grove, IL: IVP Academic, 2014.

Oz, Amos. *Dear Zealots: Letters from a Divided Land*. New York: Mariner, 2018.

Paget, James Carleton, and Joachim Schaper. *From the Beginnings to 600*. Vol. 1 of *The New Cambridge History of the Bible*. Cambridge: Cambridge University Press, 2017.

Pinker, Steven. *Enlightenment Now: The Case for Reason, Science, Humanism, and Progress*. New York: Penguin, 2018.

Plato. *Great Dialogues of Plato*. New York: Mentor, 1956.

———. *Plato's Republic*. Book 2. Translated by Benjamin Jowett. N.p., 1871.

Polkinghorne, John. *The God of Hope and the End of the World*. New Haven: Yale University Press, 2002.

Rhee, Helen. *Early Christian Literature: Christ and Culture in the Second and Third Centuries*. London: Routledge, 2005.

Rovelli, Carlo. *Seven Brief Lessons on Physics*. New York: Riverhead, 2016.

Rufinus. *A Commentary on the Apostles' Creed*. Translated by W. H. Fremantle. In vol. 3 of *The Nicene and Post-Nicene Fathers*, 2nd ser. Edited by Philip Schaff and Henry Wace. Peabody: Hendrickson, 2004.

Russell, Peter. *From Science to God*. Novato, CA: New World Library, 2002.

Sacks, Jonathan. *The Dignity of Difference: How to Avoid the Clash of Civilizations*. New York: Bloomsbury, 2003.

———. *The Great Partnership: Science, Religion, and the Search for Meaning*. New York: Schocken, 2011.

Schwarz, Christian A. *Paradigm Shift in the Church*. Carol Stream, IL: Churchsmart, 1999.

Silva, Moisés. *Biblical Words and Their Meaning*. Grand Rapids: Zondervan, 1994.

Smith, James K. A. *Desiring the Kingdom*. Grand Rapids: Baker Academic, 2009.

BIBLIOGRAPHY

Smith, Julien C. H. *Paul and the Good Life: Transformation and Citizenship in the Commonwealth of God*. Waco, TX: Baylor University Press, 2020.

Sparks, Kenton L. *Sacred Word Broken Word: Biblical Authority and the Dark Side of Scripture*. Grand Rapids: Eerdmans, 2012.

Tertullian. *Against Praxeas*. Translated by Peter Holmes. In vol. 3 of *The Ante-Nicene Fathers*. Edited by Alexander Roberts and James Donaldson. Peabody: Hendrickson, 1994.

———. *Treatise on the Soul*. Translated by Peter Holmes. In vol. 3 of *The Ante-Nicene Fathers*. Edited by Alexander Roberts and James Donaldson. Peabody: Hendrickson, 1994.

Theophilus. *Theophilus to Autolycus*. Translated by Marcus Dods. In vol. 2 of *The Ante-Nicene Fathers*. Edited by Alexander Roberts and James Donaldson. Peabody: Hendrickson, 1994.

Thorsen, Don. *The Wesleyan Quadrilateral*. Lexington, KY: Emeth, 2005.

Thurman, Howard. *Jesus and the Disinherited*. Boston: Beacon, 1996.

Tillich, Paul. *The Shaking of the Foundations*. Eugene, OR: Wipf & Stock, 1948.

Todd, Peter B. *The Individuation of God: Integrating Science and Religion*. Asheville, NC: Chiron, 2017.

Von Wyrick, Stephen. "Dynasty That Ruled Jews from the 160s to 63 BCE." In *Eerdmans Dictionary of the Bible*, edited by David Noel Freedman. Grand Rapids: Eerdmans, 2000.

Walton, John H. *The Lost World of Adam and Eve*. Downers Grove, IL: IVP Academic, 2015.

———. *The Lost World of Genesis One*. Downers Grove, IL: IVP Academic, 2009.

Weber, Hans-Ruedi. *The Cross: Tradition and Interpretation*. Grand Rapids: Eerdmans, 1975.

Wesley, John. *Sermons IV (115–151)*. Vol. 4 of *The Works of John Wesley*, edited by Albert C. Outler. Nashville: Abingdon, 1984.

Wilber, Ken. *The Religion of Tomorrow: A Vision for the Future of the Great Traditions*. Boulder, CO: Shambhala, 2017.

Witherington, Ben. *The Paul Quest: The Renewed Search for the Jew of Tarsus*. Downers Grove, IL: InterVarsity, 1998.

World Population Review. "Most Christian Countries 2025." https://worldpopulationreview.com/country-rankings/most-christian-countries.

Wright, N. T. *Paul*. Minneapolis: Fortress, 1989.

Wright, Robert. *The Evolution of God*. New York: Little, Brown, 2010.

Yoder, John Howard. *The Politics of Jesus*. Grand Rapids: Eerdmans, 1994.

Young, Brad H. *Jesus: The Jewish Theologian*. Grand Rapids: Baker Academic, 1995.

Zurlo, Gina A., et al. "World Christianity 2025: Regional Perspectives." *International Bulletin of Christian Research* 49 (2024). https://doi.org/10.1177/23969393241283291.

www.ingramcontent.com/pod-product-compliance
Lightning Source LLC
Chambersburg PA
CBHW072146160426
43197CB00012B/2263